AF395426

state of mind

beyond present

FSC
www.fsc.org
MIX
Papper från
ansvarsfulla källor
Paper from
responsible sources
FSC® C105338

intro

At this very moment, I'm realizing the truth of me surely exposing myself in such naked and harsh way, thinking to myself, this is wonderfully magnificent.
I've decided to share, upset, disappoint, delight, cherish and hurt one or another within this masterpiece. I've also decided to be honest, fragile and loving.

This book is not about doing right or wrong, or being right or wrong, it is about being and it is about the reality. It will get messy and kind of all over the place and that is simply the point. Feelings and emotions are messy and therefore this book becomes messy, and not just a little bit, quite a lot and throughout the whole book pretty much. Just a heads up.

However, preferably you must not enjoy reading it, you must not continue, but instead interpret, sense and let your physique process every word. Also, at the end of the day, you do you, you could also put the book in the bin and that would be completely alright to me. Up to you. Last but not least, I do wish for you to maintain a pleasant reading with lots of tears, laughter and madness included.

Förlag: BoD - Books on Demand, Stockholm,
Sverige
Tryck: BoD – Books on Demand, Norderstedt,
Tyskland
ISBN: 978-91-8057-298-9

dedicated to our mankind and to human beings with feelings

part 1

fear, hatred, overwhelm, disorientation,
disorganisation, misery

1

Resentment. Destruction. Boldness. Everything feels disappeared. Everything is fucked up. Everything is far beyond my comprehension. The world is consumed. I am consumed. I need to see the light but I do not want to. I want to be in another dimension and time. But I can not. I am expired. Light or dark, cold or warm, empty or full, I will always sense fear and heartache.

Flattering, innocent birds tweets and whistles outside my window while the fresh sea spring air breeze sends regards to my lungs and my body and my mind and soul. The rush of air blows my mind. I am addicted already. The sunshine explores my dark-stoned window sill through the curtains seeking for my attention. However, I will not give my permission. Winds and the sunlight suddenly, quickly abandon me. Someone is afoot wandering with their almost unnoticeable footsteps towards my bedroom door.
My room is crowded with boiled up emotions, sensations and it gets dark. Black and white. My head. My hand. My eyes. My mother,

reaches for my head, my hand and my eyes.
The sky introduces an arranged meeting for
the abundant clouds to release rain and
thunder, my desires are fulfilled.
My mind is empty with words. I answer with a
numb glance at my window.
She searches for an answer by starring into my
eyes, but it is undeniably difficult.
As the door closes, I sense the atmosphere
becoming very isolated. Non-social. All by
myself, philosophising beyond reality,
imagining the world upside down. Imagining
myself in a bubble above the stars and in a
place where nothing matters. Where I can
breathe and be present. Imagining my mind of
chaos functioning as a devil against my soul
which conceives yet another reflection that
again and again, every single day of action
brings me damage.

2

Every goddamn organism breathing is beyond lighted and alive. Every goddamn creature appears as if they already lived. Every goddamn human being is imperceptible to me. Yet I experience impressions and reflections making me the greatest departed heartbeat on earth. However, existence proofs me wrong and life will not choke me which all of a sudden eliminates my overall target within my psyche. My instinct and spirit that thrives for the conclusion of me being entirely erupted, slashed and destroyed within minutes. Within seconds. The magnificent fundamentals within my body are demanding change, pain, suffer, revenge, truth and hatred. My body capitulates. My mind sabotages. My soul transforms. Each and every section of my body screams for the universe to convert me into a concealed unreal mortal, dwelling of misery and sorrow.

Flavoured salty tears slithers down my flushed rosy cheeks from all the consumed alcohol, transforming me to an insufficient human being, according to my mind. Thrilling

according to my head. Fucked up, naive, tragic
spinning world for what? For who? Why?
WHY?
WHY?
WHY?

3

Rapidly, I choose to allow heavy music to radiate and stream through my system which with its tunes creates collateral energy within me. The harmony from the music allows me the freedom to sense acceptance and to feel comfort among my own presence. I demand wickedness. I demand perfect imperfection. Nobody cares. Nobody listens. Nobody determines for our justice to flourish and thrive. I am fragile. I am incomplete. I am annihilated, far from home. Where is home? I am far from home. While tenderly making an effortless effort to approach my legs, knees and toes helping me to have the ability and strength to rise up, I acknowledge my breathing, inhaling, infrequently exhaling becoming adequately vivid. My heart beats fast. My head twirls and spins madly and I sense vomit will emerge. However, I will not accept for it to happen, I want to go outside.

As I am squeezing my eyes being spotted by sunlight, daylight and fresh air I get into action, I move ridiculously calm. Indeed, one hell of an awful feeling. I am not convinced. I

am not satisfied. I am not ready. I am
frightened, jacked up.

Tree crowns. Looks dangerous. Yet
marvellously life depending. Strange. Cautious
birds expresses their morning spirit through
their voices. The shades of nature makes me
dizzy and safe. It is glorifying how
supernatural and yet evil the life of mother
nature doubtlessly is. Life kills life. An endless
era of slaughter. Kill. Kill. Kill. How beautiful.
What is life and for what desire and purpose
do we exist? For what purpose do we breathe?
Do we deserve life? Why are we here? Why?
Why are human beings entirely different, yet
still reflections of one another? When is the
end? Why am I still present among this
universe? Among this spinning sphere, green
and blue, black and yellow still fighting for life.
Why? Why am I here?
WHY?
WHY?
WHY?

The pain I carry evolves into rage and fear
inside and it starts controlling me, screaming at
me. Yet I could not afford to be heard, to be
seen, acknowledged. I demand for my heart to
be destroyed and my brain to get wrecked, and
my mind and soul to fade away. Life is

wonderfully miscellaneous. Magnificently odd
and foreign. Secretive.
I proceed to walk forward, through wind and
sunshine discovering an overwhelmingly
moderate piece of view from a rock sitting
down while gazing over the sea. I wish I could
say it was astonishing.

Heart is in charge. It beats similarly to a freak.
My body temperature rises as if I were to be
placed within the engines on Titanic. I then
peek at the imperfectly organic view of the sea
and I sense acceptance for my lungs to
breathe. I sense acceptance for my
vulnerability to show through watery eyes and
restless legs while being psychologically fatal.
Suddenly, while smelling a combination of
fresh soil and warmed up cliffs heated by the
shining sun I realize the very emptiness within
me passionately thirsting for food. At the same
time I force my myself to not admit the
starvation of mine. I warrant myself into
abstain from every desirable need for
remaining in this world.

Anxiety hits me. As if the very roots beneath
the flesh and bones of mine were to become
an absolute abysm. As if entirety were nothing
but an endless path of utter destruction.
Further more, why do humans have the

authority in ruling our planet? Why did such arrogant piece of organisms ever get the honour to be established on earth? In today's world, we are challenging a nightmare, misery, non indulgent souls which always, likely end up existing behind a microphone reaching millions of thousands of humans convinced by the naive, irresponsible, senseless words of him or her. Brainless bastards. Even more extraneous, the organisms behind a (motherf****ing) microphone have the extraordinary freedom in assembling our horrid piece of society. What array of humankind civilisation are we conscious in? Where is all the deliberations about uniting humans no matter what religion or ethnicity they belong to, no matter what language you express yourself through, no matter your skin colour or visual examination we should accept and respect each other? Where? When? Why? It is remarkably baffling to me. All of it. My mind is convoluted, overwhelmed by impressions and philosophies and theories there is, devastated by the arrogance among humanity, mentally disorientated because of the eternal growth of uncontrollable abundant voices in my head, telling me the worst significant pieces of information one could ever knowledge and be a part of. While my head swirls I seize my moms gaze when

stepping forward through the front door
expecting a consciously odd gaze from myself
saying more than a thousand words.
Unquestionably I select my final destination
back from the walk and undeniably it ends up
being my very personal dead room. The place
to completely be all by myself doing whatever
I want to do. The place to feel safe. The place
to be free. Free from every imaginable obstacle
and burden. Allow me to be. Just be.

4

I am laying in this bed waiting for disappointment not only from me but my parents, my whole environment. Cause it speaks to me every goddamn day. You are not enough. You are worthless. You are nothing. Stop trying. Stop seeing. Stop sensing. Stop being. Stop breathing. Stop living.

A woman in drooping, casual clothes walks up on me. She appears lightly. I tenderly putting on a slightly lively expression. She locates her confined narrow feet one by one, one after another as we wander through a mentally threatening hallway making me feel very uncomfortable. As we walk, other doors are widely accessible where psychologists and therapists hints with an awfully penetrating sort of smirking expression as I am passing by. Every millionth section of me wants to go back to my free place at home. I do not want to be here. I do not want to see this human being, calling herself a therapist. I refuse to be here. I am already aware that I will eventually ending up consuming and cracking tens of tons of unfamiliar capsules only making everything

even more widely condemned and outrageous.
Fucking brilliant.

I can not let myself breath in this disgusting
environment. The fundamental questions of
hers makes me dizzy in this ridiculously harsh
room that has no fucking air in it. My blood
pressure surges and streams through the
broken figure of mine transforming my cheeks
to appear blushed. I feel ashamed, wretched, I
feel tenacious and clingy. At the same time
wondering why my parents took me here. Why
am I here? I hate myself for making them feel
in a way that they had to take me to this place,
confronting not only myself but to them, to a
therapist. I am the reason. I am the reason I
am fucked up. I could not reply or justify. I am
not capable of it. I am not persuasive enough.
I am devoted to serenity and tranquility just
sitting in the room as if the room were
abandoned.

My delicately aroused mother speaks with an
acid voice.
Can I have a cigarette? I ask.
I leave them alone. I leave the room. I see a
small balcony and it is almost like it is waiting
for me to be stepped on to have my cigarette.
It is talking to me. Last inhale of that life
changing tobacco and I am back in the room.

I act naive, ignorant and unsophisticated. I
shut my eyelids, obstructing my ears, squeezing
and forcing my feet to make physical contact
with the completely futile couch and lastly
locating my hands on my face. I scream. I am
screaming and howling, crying and screaming.
I scream.
Unpleasantly according to my parents gaze,
frightening according to the doctors response.
My mother and the doctor keeps on having
this conversation while all I could ever think of
is getting out of here. That is all I want. I want
to be anywhere but here. I want to get out of
here. I zoom out.

5

I pray, truly pray for my mind and soul to be adept of being present within another dimension and world, within another time and place, another present time. I am beseeching and pleading, calling upon for help to find me. Guidance and love to find me. The lost and never found. Me. Presently, I am arranged and available and prepared for each desirable provocation and incitement being offered to me in order to extent the very end of me in whatever design and shape it will be presented. Endlessly and eternally. I am awaiting for our abominable society to burst, to split and explode into a million little pieces, into vanished souls and bodies all in one wonderful disorder and chaos. I am wishing for a sheer marvellous end where every bit of organism, within the wild, the supernatural and within the present existence gets affected by the intention and aim of truly pursuing an excelling life and growth where being present and available and grateful and loving are in the centre of attraction. I do not care about belongings, THINGS which carries and transports nothing but physical objects defining

and meaning unquestionably, precisely
NOTHING. Nothing. Nothing at all.

6

14th of June, another sunrise, another day and its light. As my eyes awakens, my legs shakes to prepare for everything this day has to offer, and my brain sheerly develops into this mood which includes senses and thoughts and beliefs that today is all about fearing myself, destroying myself. I sensed it the moment I woke up and it does not even bother me. Also, it is fucking ridiculous how one person in this world beliefs she will help me with her existence of nonsense with her undeniably social norm related process of work with evolving me into some kind of "normal" person in this society which other human beings will appreciate, of course, because what people want is normal, simple, copies of each other, segregation which to me means ugliness, death to our mind and souls, confusion, an era of conservatism; plastic, fake society, plastic, fake human beings walking around being extremely non attractive in any kind of way. It is ugly as fuck. Unattractive as fuck, ridiculously grisly, embarrassing. Look at how our world evolves and develops. I sense and experience sadness among a lot of people every day, both familiar and strangers who with their blank eyes tell me everything I need to know about them. Their souls are in their eyes. Their struggles and obstacles shown through their way of being, way of expressing their selfs, way of appearing to other people, way of seeing their world, our world. Our mind is our source to existence, our will to exist. People looses their minds. Some of them wants to, some of them do not know they have already lost their mind. Some of us already know but do not bother to do anything about it. I am one of them.

7

It is dazzling and pleasing how I do not recognise myself anymore. This atmosphere with cigarette smelling walls and ceilings, empty fulled apartment in the middle of the hipster's square, feeling utterly alone yet still crowded around the emptiness. I feel allowed like never before to actually and really express my feelings and emotions where no one hears me, no one sees me, no one recognises me. I am new to them, I am a foreign. Suddenly I feel free. Free to exist with no one around me. Is that alright? Alright. Then leave me alone for a few minutes. Please.

I am incapable of being around other humans. Being social. Being present. Being around other people. I can not. I can not breathe around people. People frightens me. People demands, they expect, react, talk, walk, looks at you, stare at you, scans you. People exist. But not in an enjoyable way. People destroys humanity. Humanity transforms our world into an underground. Cherishing people is erroneous. People hurt other people. It seems to be an instinct throbbing other people, making them perceive ache and soreness. Making them remember and put thoroughly on their mind a specific situation or mention causing an infinite pain which therefore causes one joining the dark, joining soreness, joining "what's not there". People are frightening and as far as I am concerned I seem to frighten people as well.

8

I started dazzling at a book cover. I gave the words a slight glance and I started to barely read as well. I peaked at the ending and then I realised I believed this is more than just a book, more than words. Although all I see is letters, commas, capital letters, small letters, dots and question marks. I have read before, but mostly for another reason, to please someone else and make another person proud. That is what school does to you. This one however feels different. Reading, is to me extremely individual and personal, especially when it comes to finding the rare time and place and peace to do so and to intimately enjoy the book. That is all it is about, coming to peace and let the words escape into your mind. To let the story become something else to one than "just a story", because there is always something else behind that book cover, behind every page, just read carefully and you will see it. Or you will not. That is when you start realizing, is it just a book or is it more than that?

This day, cloudy as hell, reckless and weak, I want to read. In fact that is all I want to do right now, maybe even put some gin in my coke when nobody is around.

9

Sunlight. Where everything allows to be observed and discovered, making every wretched truth suddenly being putted on the display among a lot of other even more ugly truths and they suddenly appear undeniably clearly. In sunlight, every bit of detail, wonderful or not, shows so innocently, perfectly fine to a point it seems supernatural. With sunlight it presents everything as we would to be in an everyday fairytale of melancholy and miserable souls walking around, dead yet still alive. Their brains collapse, their hearts were heartbroken, their bodies could not move. So what? Yet, still they are here. Currently, staring at human beings walking past the rotten park bench I without hesitation wanted to try out, sit on it, lay down on it. Collapse on it. Oh, and I just did. Then, unremarkably I woke up. Poured myself another glass of red wine. It is brilliant and sensationally beautiful how innocent these leaves look because of the sunlight. Everything looks so alive, thriving, the trees looks young and playful, the grass swirls and gets fitted by the wind appearing as the seaweed on the very bottom of the ocean among an infinity of sparkling life. Life. Life. Life. Where is all this life coming from? How do you live such life? How do you create such life? I want to know, I want to be apart of it. But also I don not, I do not want to be a part of something beautiful, because that would be a lie. I want to miserably pause and stay at this bench looking at the very refinements of life but I don not want be a part of it. How come inhaling and exhaling would be such explicit thing? How come eyes are so beautiful? How come souls and minds thrives as nature would see it. Because everybody have them, everybody carries it, everybody do it to hit life. To survive we inhale and exhale, to see and experience, see another soul we have eyes, to connect and present yourself we have our mind and soul. You could stare into someones eyes on the subway, stare at the environment, stare at yourself and suddenly you will see this world no one could ever show you but yourself. Sunlight exposes everything. Sunlight hits us different. Sunlight is not just sunlight. To me its remarkably intimidating, because it shows everything and even if you were to do exactly everything in your power to force it not to reveal the truth it will someday, somehow anyways. Sunlight, the truth.

10

Mid-May. Drugs. Wine. Living at clubs. First best choice of a person, let's go for it. All day and every day, because what else would be more important? What else could matter more than getting destroyed and ripped? Give me time and space, allow me to be me, stop interrupting, do not come near me, stop overacting, stop looking at me, don not spend time with me. Leave me alone. I am staring at myself in the mirror. At the same time I am thinking, well if not today, then when? I do not know what happens tomorrow.

I have an illusion, I have a vision, I am dreaming of going somewhere I have never been. I am dreaming of not being able to see anything, to not being able to breath or feel. Still I want to exist, for me. For me to experience chosen choices of experiencing something unhappen. I want to experience something I never thought I would, something meaningless yet rememberable. I want something different because then it feels right and it would feel like it belongs to me and myself, no one else, because that simply does not matter at all. What you think or anybody else. What I am choosing right now is not anything I regret. It is rather something speaking to me, telling me to open up and be patient and overall "not in control" for anything because that creates obstacles. Obstacles is the way to go but it does not have be involved in every move I make. However, somehow it still shows up in every possible situation. I believe something or someone is trying to tell me or show me this specific other opportunity. However, today I choose not to listen or even acknowledge it. Because why would I? Why would anybody listen to it?

Is it worth losing yourself? Is it worth giving up my whole self, life depending tools and support from others, thinking clearly, being mindful and gentle whenever its mostly needed for myself? Yes, I do think its worth it, because I can not see it another way, I would not and I am not going to.

Yet, there are voices trying to take me to places. There are meanings and thoughts and connections and pathways I have never seen before. But now, they are right in front of me. But I can not think clearly because if I were to do so, I am afraid I will see what I don not want to see. I am scared to reveal myself. I am frightened to look at me. To see me. To understand me. But most of all to change me. However, I want to believe in change, I want to make sacrifices, I want to take risks, tens and thousands of them. I am willing to put myself out there, even on the streets if that is necessary. I want perspective and I m willing to let it be presented to me. I do not know if today is the day. But I am starting to get sick of myself. Sick of being someone I don not even know and do not even recognise. I am not a person anymore. I am an enemy and I keeps hurting me, hurting others, hurting everyone. I want to change. I want to become a person.

11

February 1st. Something. Something. Something. Not at all, what I wanted to say was this. Dynamic. Stubborn. Aware. Willing. Brave. Suddenly I noticed something happening around me, I noticed something taking place and it seems strange, because when was the last time I even noticed anything. Noticed anyone. It is scary looking at people, especially when they are gazing back in a way I feel eaten up by his or her eyes. At the same time I feel thrilled staring at other people, how their feet crosses the road, how they expresses their faces, some of them looks like they need to take a shit, but some of them are easily inhaling and breathing the air so innocently it starts to get upsetting. Because how can one human being present herself humble as a bumble bee in a tree feeling that free? However, some of them passing by features agony, jealousy, anxiety, off trap expressions one could never understand if not grabbing them, holding them, offering them a strong as hell cup of coffee with a lot of sugar and ask them right up in their eyes, what the hell is wrong with you? Usually, human beings communicates and reveals their biggest fears, bringing up experiences, specific experiences from that day or even from years ago and declares about mistakes they have made throughout their everyday life which will always be there with them and follow them unless you do as Micheal Jackson once wrote for his song and simply look at the "man in the mirror" and find a way out of the hamster wheel. Look at yourself, feel yourself, express yourself, experience yourself, the answer is there and will always be there. I figured that is what I wanted to do. This day I know that whatever kind of pill it is, whatever kind of bottle of wine, whatever chat I will have with a close one, it does not matter because I need myself to be honest with myself, and that is all. To some of you out there, this theory may seem disgustingly egocentric. Disgustingly egocentric and awfully ugly because what would life be without 200 million watches and vacation trips to Maldives? That's just it, it would be everything. I want to travel within me, my soul and personality, who am I? Astonishing. Marvellous. Respect. Acceptance. Words and words and words, making me understand, making me become human. My home is myself, my needs is a priority, a place is just a place, a house is just a house, a glass of wine is, unfortunately, just a glass of wine. My body is my temple, as one of the greatest most experienced logician and philosopher, woman I have ever met, once said. Connection and absence. Most powerful experienced emotions to be presented in this spinning son of a sphere, blue and white, green and yellow. To connect and to disconnect. What else? Glass of wine, not because I have to, because I want to, it brings me relief, it brings me joy. Dangerous but needed. I connect with emotions, how do you connect? I connect with the power of love, meaning, wanting to let my hand help another hand in need. I connect by seeing. I connect by noticing. I connect by experiencing. I disconnect with "I do not have time", planning, perfectionism, "the best, the most". I disconnect with myself sometimes as well. Most importantly I disconnect with control and being told what to do. Being in control is sane and sometimes sane could be frightening and a bit overwhelming. Because there is already enough sanity in this world. There is already enough rules and expectations, demands and having everything in control. It is not sane to stay that sane.

12

What if the world was different? What if the world offered something else? Offered newness? When thinking about this, the only answer seems to be me, you and everybody else out there. I believe we live in our own world with our own responsibilities, our own abilities and principles. I also believe in our human intelligence and strength that we are capable of sharing our worlds and sharing our love. The earth did not make us come here for no reason at all. Whoever, whatever, whenever our planet was invented each one of us were born with integrity, not to be important to someone else but for me myself and for you, yourself. It was not made for the people or for the society, it was meant to be for the individual human and the individual human only. Our brains developed to learn, our heart to open up, our mind to imagine endlessly, our soul to breathe and connect, our feeling of fear to know where we feel safe and not, our feeling of joy to ultimately be present and to let some of the things go. At the very end of the day every human being shall think of the moment having a coffee with your mother, reading the extraordinary book you just started reading and will not stop reading because it is simply impossible, walking on the country field, waking up, helping one in need, watching the sunset or sunrise, having a carbonara every now and then. Because these things creates memories, valuable moments and something to remember. These experiences matter and these experiences should be in focus. However, letting one chase after what is theirs, after what one believe belongs to them, is aimed for them, is told to heal and protect one's mind and body should also be the focus. Doing what genuinely appears light as well as heavy. Doing what seems difficult yet possible is the way to go. Focusing on letting one's breath blow away, one's body collapse and then rise up, focusing on one's inner strength to show through whatever one does or goes. Life is endless, en era of infinity yet largely limited. That is it.

part ll

flourish, comprehension,
serenity, belief, stillness

1

Are we choosing to be surrounded by people we do not enjoy being around? Yes. Are we allowing ourselves to be our most genuine horrific enemy? Yes. Are we participating in creating a wonderful moment into something unworthy? Yes. But why? Why would anybody want to accomplish this just wasting time? Because, we are blind to ourselves, blind to our reality, what is happening, what is about to come. However, we can not always be prepared for everything to come, it is utterly impossible, but we could slowly, carefully, mindfully be aware of what we are doing in that very moment or in that specific hour of time having a coffee with somebody who wastes your time. I believe we have to see our very own truth, to understand where every situation and every choice leads. Remember, the hardest, yet most meaningful choice is the way to go. One must go through a sort of pain, suffer and to experience real patience to actually go for the hard way because at the end of the day one will realize that is the only way, not just a way. Also, think about the choices you make for yourself. I learned that a hesitant response to someone asking you to come somewhere or do something is a fuck no. Simply, if it is not a "fuck yes" then it is a "fuck no". Therefore, to carry this in your mind everyday, actually caring about the choices you make, the words you let through your head and your mouth plays a big fucking role to how you feel at the end of your day, during your day, at the very early stage of your day. People keep talking about putting their phone away before 11 pm, they tell you to stop eating at the latest of 7pm in the evening to not feel "bloated" in the morning, or caring so much about the way you look and your weight that suddenly "you don not have another choice than to just do it". People tell you to workout at least 60 minutes a day, to not drink coffee and also don not eat too much vegetables because then you will fart a lot. But also don not eat fast food because that will make you look fat. All these assumptions, comments, beliefs we are just supposed to believe because of the ugly reason; "everybody" else believes in it so why would I not believe in it as well. Well, I am here to tell you people are here to fuck with your mind through social media and their business to earn money. Money and fame. Money and manipulation. Money and grief. Beautiful, very beautiful. That is apparently what everybody seems to think in this world.

We are human beings, what happened with knowing ourselves, taking care of ourselves, taking care of others you love not others who you don not give a fuck about because those people are not important. What happened with giving a shit about the things you care about and not for the reason of making money, getting more and more stuff, eating at fancy restaurants or staying at expensive hotels. It will get you nowhere right now and it will not ever get you anywhere for that matter. You will be a loser at a hotel room by yourself not hearing from your family, relatives, the real world. You will end up in an armchair putting a bullet in your head because you are thinking to yourself, what the fuck matters in this life? And you question yourself so much you do not even know the answer anymore. Because what used to matter when you were a child is now liquids, hotels and chicks. One choice leads to another and before you know it you are someone you do not recognise. Almost, speaking about myself you may think and the truth is, yes, I do, I mean, I did live that way.

2

I have been thinking about life. What do I want from it? How do I want to live my life? How do I want to live my life without anyone else's thoughts or theories, because those are their theories, not mine so I do not listen to them. Sometimes if it is an encouraging, loving or supportive comment or advice from another soul, I would probably think about it, but still that is not my final choice just because it sounded intelligent or logic. Because as soon as I discover my way of living and make it a constant journey, there is never a start or an ending, according to me, it is always a movement in some sort of way, it will sound logic too. Last night, I could not sleep. No matter if I relaxed my whole body, let my chin drop, my head rest against the fairly soft pillow or even when trying some breathing exercises it would not work. My head was not under control and I thought to myself, is it a fucking full moon outside? Well, did not check, however I am pretty sure this was about something else. I felt like I was communicating with myself during this point where I just got a whole bunch of different answers to my very

many questions in life. What am I prioritising?
Am I where I want to be? With people I enjoy
being around? Am I doing this for me or is it
as some point meant to be for someone else?
Did I make the right choice? And so it went
on. For at least a couple of hours thinking to
myself again, what the hell is happening. Then
I remembered this is not weird at all. I am
starting my journey, I am starting to question
my life and what really has a purpose? What
values does not? I am starting to realise why I
am here, I am simply a human being trying my
best to find comfort in myself to then be able
to show love to others and then staying that
way so that I can be grateful. I figured out, life
does not have to be a constant obstacle, you
choose if that is what you want or not. I know
it because I have been on this journey, maybe
not long enough, but enough indeed to realise
it does not have to be difficult, all the time, sure
difficulty is healthy and needed but not
difficulty only. You choose your perspective
and that becomes your everyday life. I had
these answers to my questions yesterday
because I started to release them myself, I did
not need somebody to tell me because me
myself had the answers right in front of me all
the time. Look in the mirror. It is often from
there we get our answers. So stop chasing,
wondering and asking for what is already in

front of you. Also, we are all different so of course your answers will not be the same as another's.

3

A person once said to me: I do not get you, I do not understand what you are trying to say, I do not want to understand you. And I answered, well, to "get" me is to wanting to understand one and not the opposite. She looked at me as if I were from another planet. Thinking about it today and almost every day since it happens very often to me that people "do not understand me" makes me going even further with complicated answers and descriptions which makes perfect sense to me. However, I learned that for other people it does not make sense to them and they are the ones I usually do not feel comfortable being around. It does not mean that I will simply reject them every time meeting a person not being sable to see where I come from, but I keep a balanced distance, still of course treating them with respect but I will not let them in to my space of well being. The thing about people and making sense seems to be utterly important to a seriously huge amount of people, but guess what that is not what everything has to be about. Everything does not have to have a reason or an explanation, unless one are talking about solving a murderer case. It is fine to leave it blank, or open and let the universe sometimes decide, let the time decide. It is if human beings always and always and always have to have the answer straight away. I need to know you know. I need an explanation right here right now. I need more more more and that I need now now now. First of all, to consider and comprehend the overall situation or argument you have to be in a stable, balanced, respectful state of mind to even have the energy to face what we call an answer. To make sense is not about appearance or the "right" answer or the way you react. To make sense is to take a step backward, meet the issue and then in peace and quiet, maybe with an healthy amount of sleep you could then face whatever is not making sense to you. Also, does everything need to make sense? Why does it need a reason? Think about a piece of abstract art, does it make sense? Probably not, and that my friend is the very, surely beautiful part of that lovely piece of art. But still, human beings must label it, put a meaning to it, a reason for it to be made, a price, a cost, an artist, where is it from? Who did this? Is this a famous person? Cut the bullshit. It is a painting not a real estate property.

4

Is it not admiring how ones picture of our world could change entirely from one day to another. There are days where I visually experience my environment, my world to be the most horrid and frightful vision that I ever thought it could actually be presented as. This vision includes materialistic elements, the essentials of a human and the very orally spoken words I hear storming through my ears as if I have no choice to keep it away from me wether I enjoy those words or not. Do not interpret me wrong, words are our way to communication and comprehension, however at the same time, is it really? Do we have to express ourselves in words? I vote for fucking no. Do not tell me a picture got a thousand unspoken words because I already know that and for the matter of fact it is truly something I believe in. Pictures, illustrations, paintings, photos, sketches, sculptures, music, the list is long, they all include a message, not necessarily a purpose but a message, for sure. I am also not telling you the message might be the same for you as it is for me but that is the very necessary part. Therefore, speaking with existing creativity is the most beautiful thing I have experienced. Therefore, use a wise and respectful communication around people. Words are not to be spoken sometimes but that seems to be an impossible choice for a lot of human beings in this world, destroying, tearing someone apart, a relationship, yourself to the fullest which I do not comprehend. Speak with tenderness and most importantly, awareness, otherwise you can keep your mouth shut.

5

Days. What is it about them? They are special, yet so frightening to me, because all of a sudden you are supposed to have everything figured out, everything in control. My days are ridiculously long at this very point of my life, seem to never end. How do I spend my day? How do I want to spend my day and with what purpose do I even want to get out of bed? I am constantly in thinking mode, never seem to be able to shut down, to close my eyes and let my very own dreams in deep sleep appear. Suddenly the night seems to be even more important, because I heard sleep heals my body and therefore my head. It heals whatever needs to be healed and processed and figured out. So, why will I not let my body do so? Unfortunately I have no answer and sadly that is my reality as we speak. I am repeatedly seeking for my own truth but it is hard when all I can think about is whenever I want to end the day which right now seems to be at 3 pm and at the same time I strongly believe in living for the day, the present but what if it sometimes will not be that desirable way? I want to believe that is alright but I tend to

strictly force myself into the thought of it not
being alright since I have inhumanly high
demands for myself in every corner I try to
seek for a choice or a way of thinking.

6

Crispy air, 11 degrees, sunlight, wind, speaking birds, city cars cleaning the streets from cigarettes, beer bottles, street food napkins. This is one of the most terrific mornings I have ever been around utterly presently. Having eye contact with another human being today is no problem, and certainly not with an upfront walking human coming towards me, even if he or she gazes at me in a strange way. It makes me wonder what they are thinking about and it makes me feel very calm and still and I want to laugh and I want to show people around me some intense love today, I want to show people I care about simply caring about others. This is a different day with different thoughts on my mind and it is surprising. I sense a sort of gratitude and appreciation for being able to be present among this morning that it is very hard to even put words into it. However, I will try to. The feeling of being a part of something, a part of a café during 7 am in the morning on a Saturday, a part of the streets walking from home to another destination, a part of the world being able to walk, talk and express myself however I want to express myself is an amazing feeling. I am a part of the world and the world is a part of me. Yet, still there is a lot more to see, a lot more to experience and a lot more worthy lessons and obstacles to come, and for that I am grateful because in a mind of thinking about the end throughout every second and every day the end will come, and it will come in a way one did not prepare for it to arrive. I used to think about the end a lot, even when I did not really wanted to it somehow caught my attention every time, it was not pleasant, it was not admirable but it was my reality then, because I chose to let it come and I chose to let it in my head. I chose the thoughts to brainwash my mind so that I would think in a certain way harming myself, for all that was worth. The fact is, do not always listen, but priorities and do so wisely. When feeling like something is wrong, when you feel upset, when you feel hopeless, when you feel like you have nothing to come with, listen to it wisely and listen to it with intelligence because those are not unreal, however the process begins when you choose to let it in or not. If you choose to listen to it or not. Feelings appear, thoughts appear, it is a part of the human mind and that makes it so crucial, however a feeling of thinking about the end is not beautiful and according to me, we did not arrive valuable in this world on the day we were born to only think about the end when that is the exact sign of someone who have not started their journey yet. Therefore, the journey is about arrive whenever you let it arrive.

7

Mornings. How come some of them are very easy, automatic? How come one of them feels like the biggest challenge during the whole day? To wake up or to not wake up. To rise up or not to rise up, no matter what is waiting for you during that day, or the things that are not waiting for you. The very true but very frightening part and detail of mornings, according to mine today in particular, is the conscious thought of "having" to get up, "having" to go trough today's agenda, "having" to take a shower. It sounds ridiculous. More importantly it feels utterly inappropriate to even feel this way, because "why would you not get out of bed? Why would you not start your day? However easy it may seem, some days will not be easy, it will be a challenge. It will be as if you do not want this specific morning to even take place, neither the day at all. I want to sleep this day away. I command for the consciousness to go away for a while and I wish for the time to simply disappear. I am tired of even having to check the time, keep on track of time and let it decide my day. Today I am dreaming of a reality not being in a total control and demand of always checking on the time or have a schedule even.

Today I am also thinking quite a lot about these so called "getaways", escaping from situations, relationships, a job, responsibility, consequences from ones choices etc. Now, what is it about them? It surely means something, but the question is, how far does it go or how little does it take for it to take place in ones day or ones whole life? For me, it can take an hour or 2 months, it depends if I had a good day or a bad day. Now, some may say this is called being inpatient, being unable to figure things out or to not "wait long enough" for the answers "to come to you", although I do believe in signs and the ability to wait for something called greatness. Still, I believe it is a sort of beauty in being able to truly listen to yourself, and not only yourself but your inner self, your heart and at some parts your brain, if necessary. Listening to yourself is the greatest most effective way of guidance you will ever experience. Listening to your beating heart, fighting for you everyday is a sort of way to remind you are not alone, it is there, and only for you, for you to be able to listen and make these meaningful choices everyday that leads you to either possibilities or disabilities. I believe in choosing madness, variations,

newness and curiosity, but I also believe in
balance, to listen, to stop, to reflect since these
type of processing and these two ways of
acting work like magic when being used
together. Therefore, escaping must not
happen, misery and hard times appear, for sure
and that is a part of it, however in the long run
that is the way to go. The obstacle is not in
your way, the obstacle is your solution and if
believing in solving problems instead of
running away, showing your unrealness, will
not take you anywhere but closer to "the end".
So, never mind, I will get out of bed today and
I hope you will too.

8

Is someone going to fight your fight for you? Is someone, no matter who, your friend, mom, a guy from the coffeeshop going to save you from whatever is stopping you from being you? The answer is shockingly, to some people, no. It was even for me once upon a time. I did not believe in the world being made to "save" me, but I did believe in the world solving my problems through materialistic objects, people pleasing relationships, fitting in etc. No wonder I had a hard time with being respectful to myself when there was no time to feel in any such way since "all of the other" parts of my day were in my way. Waste of time. Waste of days. Waste of everything that offers to you in this world, still it was crucial to then become different. I remember my days in high school undoubtedly clear and precisely. I even remember specific parts of the days, lessons, hours and the minutes before walking to the train station to take me to my home. But mostly I remember the relationships, the social parts of school not being able to be me, because I simply did not think anyone would ever want to meet me, the exact way I am, the exact way I think and appear. I simply walked around with a ridiculously heavy, carrying wall in front of me, screaming inside of wanting to smash that wall to the ground and show the real me. However, that was impossible. Right? It was impossible when I would not let myself. The most interesting part here is the reason. Why? Why would I not show me? Act the way I act? I was afraid and I was not brave, I was in an utterly dangerous way of thinking that everybody, even the teachers and the assistants were against me, always. I thought in a way it only harmed myself. I saw my side of the story, but what about the true story? The reality. Their stories? However, one day I started to question things, I started playing with my thoughts, I started to move around with my thoughts and let them slowly, carefully they got showed and told to another humans consciousness and yes, I continued to do so. I continued and very soon, it was as if nothing were really impossible, it was an episode, a part of my life, however I realised it was not someone else, it was not a specific event that caused me to think that way. It was me. All me, all the time. I did not exactly choose to think this way but all that is needed to continue to think this way is if you start believing in it and suddenly it becomes a pattern, a lifestyle, an everyday life kind of situation where it then leads to a "personality". But for me, it was all a wall of lies. It came natural to me. I went from a "fictionally", unreal way of being into a completely living spirit, expressing myself, choosing freedom over limitation. Choosing to be different, to think differently. To act differently and then never stop thinking differently.

9

Presently I am sipping on a chunk mug of american coffee knowing that I will soon start shaking and maybe crying, perhaps pee myself or even worse, not being able to think clear. I am sensing the anxiety already, trying to be smooth, sneaking up on me, and it reaches my full attention. I watch people around me searching for trattorias, trips to the beautiful outside world of Florence, tourists walking with these horrific sticks they use to take a photo of themselves. Embarrassing. Grab a coffee instead. An enormous dark, filthy, thirsty cloud builds up just above me and it feels like I am going nuts. I am afraid this is the point where I am starting to achieve those feeling of actually being present, of actually thinking of what I am consuming, putting in to my body, of actually thinking about what I let go through my head and what I will not let go through my head. It is overwhelming to be this present. To be present among other people who does not seem to be present at all. I stare at the woman in the cashier, the barista who makes coffee, every single movement, every single costumer she is helping, every single child coming in with their mom or dad holding their hands getting to choose whatever they want from all the glorious pastries offered not feeling guilty or worried or unhesitant at all. It is scary how much one notices when taking the time to notice. I sense the air become foggy, the windows goes frosty and the outside seems to be ridiculously stressful. It is just a city, some may think. It is a city full of light and life and love and food and people, however it is not enough because all of these elements does not show anymore. Where is the peace and quiet and where are the people with a slightest, most tender way of being? Is this our society? Is this the way we are suppose to live? Jacked up, stressed, overwhelmed, anxious, unhappy, disgraceful. I am a part of it but I choose not to be. I want to choose not to be. Letting something reach me, reach my attention, reach my inner space will not be possible for anyone who is not willing to be present. I choose something else, but I do not know what exactly.

In and out. Up and down. Side to side. No, I am not talking about something intimate, I am talking about the way we behave every single day. What we let in, what we let out or not let out, what are our ups and what are our downs? Should we move in another direction? Should we keep going the way and path we have chosen to be walking or not? Should we run our path or should we slowly get here? As our days goes on, everything else goes on. Rivers and waterfalls, city traffic, walking people, women giving birth and so on. The world keeps spinning, the sun goes up and it goes down, the wind changes direction through the day, sometimes it disappears, sometimes appears. The rain will fall or it will not. Everything goes on, we are in a constant movement. That means everything we choose, where we walk, what we eat, what we choose, who we are spending time with, what we choose to say and not to say will at some point show and it will be a true way of showing your habits and your beliefs and your simple way of being. Eating, consuming and acting are the biggest to be shown which is why those specific parts of your day are inherently important and must be prioritised and for some, reconsidered. Your body is your temple and so do not let the devils on the other side take that from you. It is yours and yours only. Your food, your choice. Your way of consuming, your choice. Your preferred way of being and spending your time. Your choice. No one else is choosing this but you and so take care of that magnificent opportunity and ability you are carrying everyday, because if it will not be carried and be a part of your day today it will suddenly lead to consequences you do not desire and there will be grief, regrets and anger. Still these are parts of our lives and must be to know where the no's are and where the yes's are, However, to constantly carry a bag of anger and grief will be heavy and it will be a heavy ride. Let your choices matter and let them matter to you, no one else. What you choose today will show tomorrow, and the next week, even a year from now. Therefore, value the present and let the choices be your path, because the choices simply lead you to everything to come.

11

The older I get, the more I think of myself as a child. I think of my childhood and everything that included. What happened then, what I felt, experienced, learned, taught, the way I got spoken to, the way I was raised, what relationship I started and ended, kept and let go. I often let myself wonder very very carefully, in detail who I was as a child and how I spent my days, how I saw my days. I let myself remember the past to let myself move forward. The past is the past, and the past belongs to the past. However, thinking and remembering the past helps me figure out a lot about who I am right now and who I want to be. For an example, I was trying to recognise and relive moments, activities and daily habits that I used to do a lot and it came to mind directly how much of those experiences I am still living with today, things I still do and wish for it to stay that way. Going on school trips or by myself to places being outside, eating outside, enjoying the present. Today I visit the park every now and then or preferably the forest itself to have a quiet meal for myself or with any other person whom I admire to spend time talking to and spend time talking about everything life has to offer. I used to love watching people, by myself, at the schoolyard, in the park, at a restaurant with my family. I still do. I used to always want to express myself in any way by performing or singing or look myself in the mirror, incautiously talk to myself. It made me comfortable and I felt safe talking to myself a lot. These are a few examples of how I spent my days back then and it explains a lot how much it means to me doing it still since it took me to a place where I feel utterly aloud and free and comfortable right where I am. Being outside, thinking to myself, talking with myself, trying to understand myself, expressing myself, through written words or painting today, it makes me understand myself. It makes me feel aloud to be and to be me. I will keep doing these things for as long as I can until spirits or angels or devils chooses me to say goodbye to our earth. However, among these sort of patterns, or decisions, or whatever you would like to call them it is genuinely appropriate to be able to change, to be able to break those patterns, to be able to see another perspective, to see another type of "everyday". Of course I would change some of my habits, and trust me many of them have been changed, sometimes for the better but sometimes for the worse, but the point is if it makes you feel completely present and that you have the ability to do this experience a lot then it means it is a keeper, you should stick with it and for god sake do not let it go because of a person, because of a job, because of what someone else thinks, and most importantly, shockingly do not limit yourself into thinking this experience giving you hope and purpose will not be important, because it really is. It is what I call an everyday high between your everyday lows and so that specific high, specific activity, rises you whenever you need it, and when that low bastards runs in during your day, you grab your shit and go outside, grab a coffee, go for a walk, watch a movie, whatever is your happy inner space. Or as I like to call it even more, your comfort space which no one, not even your brother is allowed to get near, because it is yours only. Change is necessary, change is life dependant, change is a miracle when happening, however make sure the change will benefit you and make your way of being more meaningful, not for no reason at all and not for anybody else. For you, and for your future. Healthy habits, loving surroundings and self sufficiency are keys to being able to be fully present and to be grateful for being where you are right now, not where you were, or are going to be, because tomorrow will solve itself,

all you have to "worry" about is if your coffee
machine will work during the morning and
that you make sure the sun really did rise up.
Those are the things we can think about, the
rest is not for us to control, because we cannot.

12

Trust you instinct, I believe. Trust your thinking, not your thoughts, your thinking. Trust your inner voice and especially when being around chaos. Trust the power of being violently silent, using your voice when needed, not when being told to. Trust your journey because it will never stop trusting and following you and your choices. See and interpret, feel and think, listen and understand, choose wisely, very wisely. Imagine the thought of always being reminded of the fact that there is no one out there being the exact way you are, no one out there to be able to think the exact way you think, interpret and listen the way you listen and interpret. Therefore, we use communication, does not have to mean screaming, shouting, acting rapidly. Rather it is about seeing and hearing and listening, then it becomes quite simple to actually understand another person. However, this does not mean to accept everyone, to enjoy every persons company, to agree on every argument or point, to stay silent and pretend to enjoy the moment. No, not at all. This gives you the freedom to let yourself understand and see another side of something to then let yourself feel the exact way you want to feel about something. To let you process it in your own way and let it be a work only for you and no other purpose. We can either act with only emotions, only anger, only frustration, sadness, grief and brutality, but we can also let the thoughts run through your head, as it will, let it sink in, maybe sleep on it, go for a walk, drink some water and then come back for a reasonable answer which hopefully will not only be respectful for the other person but mostly to you for making an effort to not hurt another person. To not disrespect someone so that you then feel the anger, frustration and pain they arrived with starting the communication between you.

13

A lot of days with thunder and storm, with overwhelming ideas and feelings and it surely consumes you. It consumes you and it destroys you in the very moment. During yesterdays ultimately quiet and humble evening watching our beloved sunset and as I was listening, really listening and just watching I sensed a quiet I have never felt before, never experienced before. I felt empty. I felt full of desire and enjoyment because suddenly I was not afraid of silence anymore. On top of that I am trying utterly and authentically hard to quit my desires of smoking and even having a glass of wine before bed because it "soothes" and calms my mind. Which is bullshit. It came to mind all I need was silence and myself being put in this situation where all you can do is sit and listen and see and hear and being silent. However, it also came to mind that no place is no such place as complete silence, complete shut down of noises around us, no matter if we are home, in the forest or at a café. It is not really silent, however when not being distracted by anything, by anyone, being by yourself for hours and hours and hours that sort of silence build up on you, it built up on me and when being in these sort of moments I understand everything so deeply. I see very deeply and I see details, and I acknowledge people in a way I have never acknowledged them before. I look at this one person thinking of how he smiles, or how another woman yelling at her child for running away from her all the time, or at the man playing the violin at this Piazza in Florence who seems to be enjoying his present so much even the people around him do so as well. I sense silence around myself, when reading a book, watching the sunset, walking, but most importantly I sense silence when doing certainly and precisely nothing. Nothing at all. I remember to always have a couple, yes I said a couple, of hours a day just being and being very very, very present among that specific time of the day. Because this time of the day may be and is without doubt the most valuable, important, loving, developing, sensing, joyful part of the day where answers comes to me, where thoughts are being processed, where I can feel so utterly grateful for being a part of this world. It is as if we were to be present among our sleep, awake in our sleep, that is how soothing it feels. It is something that changes my everyday life and the best part of it, anyone can do it, in fact go ahead and take a moment

today, just you, for yourself and truly
acknowledge your surrounding, drop any
devices even if its a book or music, we do not
need anything for this period of time and just
listen. Acknowledge. Try to see and
understand your environment, not looking at it
but seeing it and interpreting what is actually
going on around you. Then, start thinking if
this is the admirable environment bringing you
a sense of safety and comfort you wish to have
in your everyday life, I am not talking about
the desire for your future and I am certainly
not talking about the past, your future and
your past is not present among us and so that
will take care of it self, believe it will and it will.
To be able to observe and witness your
environment wherever you might be located
on this earth is to see another perspective, to
improve and to help yourself become
something you never thought you could
become. Meaning, free of doubt and instead
remain a serious amount of self respect, self
discipline, to become confident. To become
self sufficient and to have the answers when
your obstacle and your problems, issues and
miseries arrive. To be present among every
present period of time, which is in fact all the
time of our days because we do only exist in
the present. It is hard to believe if you keep
fighting it, if you keep worrying about what

could happen and not what is going to happen or in fact, what is happening right now. Therefore, take your time and be present among silence. Silence and stillness will be the solution for an unimaginable number of times in your life wherever you are in your life, whatever you do or not do, no matter what age you are in, no matter your life situation. It works for human beings, people, everyone and not a certain part of the society. N matter if you are a politician, billionaire or a homeless person. When I say everyone, I mean everyone. That is what is beautiful with stillness and silence. It belongs to everyone and you decide whenever to reach out for it and whenever you need it, because it will always be there for you.

14

There is something about being alone. There is something about thinking about the time in a very unnatural yet real way. There is something about not talking to anyone in reality for a couple of weeks. There is something about being alone and that something is a frightening experience, especially when it is your very first time. I am not talking about the kind of loneliness where you ignore people because you do not feel like meeting anyone, or the loneliness where people think they are lonely because they are watching a movie all by theirselfs feeling bad for theirselfs even if being asked to come to your parents house for dinner. That is called depression. Depression is something you do not choose, something happening and your body is simply telling you to fuck off and to not be existing at all is if you have no value or no voice or even a mind, heart or body for that matter. I am talking about the loneliness you thought you knew about, that I thought I had experienced before and I thought I had been through mental pain, which I indeed have, but not in this way. Never wanting to talk to other people because it frightens you to get to know other existing people who also speaks another language, to not know even one street in the city, never being able to go to that special place at home that will forever be my special place and no one else's. To not be able to talk to my nearest friend or family, my siblings in real life for a long period of time. Suddenly I had no idea what the hell I was doing. Suddenly, nothing made sense and I felt insanely numb, confused, lost everyday and I sure did not recognise myself mentally, physically or spiritually. Where are my jokes? Where are the people I love being around? Why did I leave? And for what? How come this seemed to be the splendid and pure trip I would ever put myself through when in fact it only taught me a whole lot about what matters, what truly matters to me and what truly has a meaning in this world. It taught me patience, I learned to be strong for myself, I learned to prioritise, I learned what makes me feel cherished and protected and what does not. I learned to talk to myself and listen to myself, to stand up for myself and I learned that that was the only way. I chose to not give up this time even if this experience of being completely all by myself in a new world of culture, language, surroundings, lifestyle and all it had to offer, was the most painful and terrifying one I have

ever been through and for that I am beyond
thankful I experienced, for the cause of
knowing myself even better at this point and
knowing what is important to me, not what I
thought was important, but what indeed really
matters.

15

The fact that everything, and specifically everything can change during one day. Forget about the fact that change does not occur over one day or night or hour for just one second, even though it does not make sense right now or probably never will. All because, this day everything changed. I am going home and as I am writing this I am really, really trying not to let my tears out of my eyes because there is a baby staring at me, also there is a woman staring at me doing the coffee and the waitress stares at me every now and then because I have only ordered an Americano and been here for three hours already, how popular. Sorry for that. I am then letting teardrops fall and my computer gets all wet and I burst out giggling cause I can not control this moment and I believe this kind of moments are not supposed to be controlled at all, in fact I want this moment to be a memory in my head, a memory of true feelings and emotions coming out of my system, mostly from my heart and I believe I have been needing this for too long. Way too long because this sort of feeling I have not felt since the day I was born. This shows how much other happenings, events, grades, money, stuff and all that our beloved society has to offer does not mean shit. Because all of them will one day or another disappear, events will last for a couple of hours, money is a number on your account, stuff and objects breaks and costs you money to then be fixing what broke. But friendships, relationships and yourself is something that can not be compared, or taken for granted or to anyhow be exchanged or bought. We are a part of nature living in societies, cities, villages and farms. Lets not forget about where we came from and what were presented in front of us when we were born. Now, this starts to make sense. We were not born with an iPad in our mothers stomach, or a bank account or a job interview the next coming day after being born. We were born just the way we are without anything to it. We were born with value and dignity and love. Everybody were born with dignity, love and value. As for today, I will never forget when and where and with whom I was born with. Remembering it and keep remembering gives me clarity and sanity, it gives me a meaning and my journey starts to develop into something greater than me in a sense of me getting to know me in a way I have never thought of myself and the way I was nourished with bullshit information before.

16

The end of a semester. The end of a job. The end of a relationship. The end of a marriage, assignment, interview, coffee session, cigarette session etc etc etc. The end is such dramatic word, is it not? The end is almost aggressive and it just decides. It is a end. It just decides when it is enough and when it is time to stop. This is what is so astonishing and powerful with endings. Endings are powerful and necessary due to its very fresh, new, exciting and delicate capability of starting something else. It is the beginning of something else. It is a turn and a twist, a new goal to look forward to. A new era, a new way of thinking, a new way of appearing, a new way of being. Everything starts over and everything will be different. Let everything come to you, let everything be presented, let everything be shown and offered and then you have the power, the possibility, the ability to say yes or no, to accept or neglect, to choose something else or to stick with the offer you were given. However, it is confusing at first, because what are the choices really and how do I simply choose? How do I know if it is the "right" choice. You simply do not, because as we talked about later, the future is nowhere to be known and nowhere to be seen. We have no idea what the future offers and that is wonderful, because then it is one less worry to be anguished and concerned about. Do not let the morality be prioritised during this period of time when you have just reached an end of something that is meant to be a start of something else. Do not let fear or objection, disbelief and your insecureness fall in to place and have the control because in that way your future does not look alright and it will not bring you a development of peace. Instead, let your heart be in control and let your head be a little bit moved out of the way for a second as well. Let your heart decide and let yourself find room for your inner self and your found silence and simplicity of being among your surrounding to think. Think until you can not think anymore. Think, really think until you feel absolutely nothing. Think until you feel so utterly bare and blank and desolated that you are ready to stand up and then start writing down the first thing you think of. The very first thought or feeling or emotion or memory that you could think of. This word, this specific word will be the key to use when making your choice and when being offered anything, anything at all whatever it might be, whenever it might take place. To be starting a own company, to be offered a job, to be offered to meet a friend, to start a new relationship, to be offered to move to South Africa, to spend your day however you would wish to spend it and not to be demanded by someone else and spend it the way someone else wants you to spend it, because, because why really? When in hesitation and disorientation within your mind, even if nothing specific or enormously adventurous happened you can still use this method to simply try to clear out, fill your head with emptiness and follow whatever is in your heart telling you to go and then dare to follow it.

17

How natural yet scientifically difficult type of system and machine our head truly is and how incomprehensible that our head is dealing with all of the work it is handling and processing everyday to help us learn, repeat, function, think and believe. Tens and thousands of mechanisms and nerves and cells and smaller systems are engines to not ever get overheated even one day or another, no matter how frustrated or low and sad we can feel the engine never stops, it keeps the system going and it keeps our machine working for the next day and the rest to come. Our head but even more correctly, according to me, our mind that belongs to our heads is controlling an marvellous big part of us and therefore if we do not take care of our system of everything we own, both mentally and physically we will not function and if really underestimating it and avoiding taking care of it we will not appear in this world because our way of thinking collapse and our functioning becomes pointless and meaningless and you can only see the other side which to a lot of people is the end. To take care of our minds, our largest and greatest source of knowledge, experiences, memories and simply the chamber of everything we have ever been though since birth, I learned to remind myself of feeding it with fuel, nourishing fuel. It is very simple yet still so difficult since it is all about finding the way, not a way, and finding a balance, finding a routine, finding what works for you and finding something that makes you thrive and flourish and grow. The hardest part is yet to come, to stick with it and the even more important and essential part is believing in it, trusting every step of the way and surround yourself with this routine wherever you go, wherever you are and whoever you are with and no matter what changes or issues you meet on your journey. To benefit from right sources is to benefit a healthy mind, which benefits your way of being and the way you think about simply every living organism, existing thing around you. About our world, which in case you did not notice is your world too. It will make you think clear and with clarity and simplicity. To feed your brain with nourishing food, to communicate with truly inspiring people who are there to help not to make you shrink. To feed your brain with fresh air, walks and memorable talks with someone you admire and care about. To feed your brain with informative, supportive, clarifying books that is not really there to guide you or find the way for you because that is the persons assignment for herself to figure out. Instead feed yourself with these books that simply brings you the feeling of wanting to continue and that makes you finding an answer to your questions and helping you move forward with an issue or a life crisis that suddenly, thanks to your reading and learning and patience could have a solution for you if only time and energy are put into it as well. With that being said, non of these things will do it by itself, it is to be found among us but it is a difference between having it around us and to include it to our routines and our everyday life. Let's come up with a quite ridiculous yet very easy to handle example to clarify. When walking through a grocery store you will pass the greens, kale, spinach, broccoli, carrots, even beautiful cabbages and brussels sprouts. You then pass the shelf with chocolate, candy and marshmallows and quite the majority would absolutely, definitely go for the shelf with the sweets. Why? Does not really need to have a reason but in many cases there is this one simple reason and it goes like this. We went to the store hungry, stressed, out of thought and even with the thought of wanting to comfort ourselves to just buy some good food because I had the worst day ever possible. Or it can be like this, you simply do not think at all or mind at all, you simply do not give a fuck about anything and you choose whatever you feel like in the moment, you choose whatever would taste insanely good at that moment having no doubts or worries what it might lead to in a couple of hours or even minutes or days if that is the case. The point is, we tend to stop thinking, stop caring and stop seeing the reality due to stress, overwhelming experiences or feelings, anxiety, worries, depression and the list goes on. We act from our emotions and in an undoubtedly impulsive and disoriented way which makes us follow this routine since our routine has these elements of stress and anxiety around us all day and so it becomes a rabbit wheel of miserable decisions. Food is to be utterly the biggest source of nutrition we achieve each day and is something we allow our systems to process 3 or 4 or even 5, maybe 6 times a day depending on your needs and habits. To put only garbage in our system will evolve and show garbage in the way you behave, act and what type of choices you make since your levels in lucky feelings rises so high in a couple of minutes it makes you feel like shit after two minutes of eating that shit because, well you just ate something shitty and so you will feel shitty. However, back to balance. Cinnamon buns and candy was not made for the people to completely be ignored, however some do ignore them and I respect that fully, but we need nutrition and we need to think about what we are putting in our bodies to be able to function. Functioning to the point you become utterly in peace and true presence that makes you feel like you are truly enough and you do not have to join anything that will not make you feel good. Functioning is to be walking and to be ablate stand up and go trough your day being treated and treat others with respect and sanity. Being in this state of mind, being in a sense of stillness and comfort throughout your days allows you to have the ability to choose the right, because you give your brain fuel to do so, and you give your brain kale and spinach once in a while and fresh air to be able to conquer any person calling him the boss to run you over and over again when all you have to do is to see your everyday from a new perspective. Start with thinking about what you are adding to your mind, what foods and supplements are you adding to your brain today? How much of a time do you allow your body to breathe in fresh air and to allow your bones and flesh and muscles to get out there and move a little. Think about how much you actually take care of these parts and your mind will glorify and celebrate you with a new way of thinking and to be able to be in utter mildly presence and to be able to make your choices, not only seeing them. Make them become real and let the choices be your way out of the rabbit wheel. Because they are the way out of your miserable rabbit wheel.

18

Diffusely, I barely let my eyelids reluctantly slowly open with ultimate resistant as if the world is not ready to meet me today and the sun is is not ready to throw its golden, blinding lights on my face. Silently I lay in my bed for a couple of minutes, staring at the ceiling, staring at the blank white walls, gazing myself in the mirror beside my bed, seeing myself for the first time during this morning and something is different. I turn around to the side and now laying on the side of my body and start staring at myself and I stare for so long I observe and spot my pupils in my eyes, I can nearly but almost notice how they are getting bigger and bigger and then smaller and even smaller again. I am currently visualising this day as one of the most infinite upcoming day and clearly it frightens me, because I also sense my gut being anxious and my body starts shaking a bit and my head do not really know what to think at this very time. For a moment I sensed my legs disappear and I had to check if they were still there and now where are my hands? Where are my ears placed? Why is this dot on my stomach right here? Nothing seemed to be right or how I remembered it to be. I am uncomfortable so I try to unnoticeably leave my bed with a glance at the mirror again, staring at myself again, and I look through the window blinds if something is currently happening right outside my window or if that is just an imagination that would be absolutely beautiful if it where true. However, I acknowledge the usual, stained grey walls, old as hell and ready to fall, I acknowledge the old woman through my window in the apartment in front of me using her mocha to make coffee and her windows becomes foggy and disgusting. I then acknowledged the cat being on the roof everyday, sounding like a hurting grandmother with severe back pain, crying like a baby and no one seems to own it or take care of it. What is it with todays spirit? Suddenly, showering seems very strange and putting clothes on would be mad insane. Having breakfast? What is breakfast even? Coffee? No thanks. I am staring at myself in the mirror again. I have changed and I am scared. I notice I am suddenly capable of letting myself stare at my self, scanning myself, seeing through myself at a ridiculous long amount of time and since I am all alone it does not feel weird. I peek and glance at my dull skin, my dead cheeks, sloppy legs and poisoned posture. At the same time, at this point I do not want to see myself that way, I am not the same person as I were before. I am not letting this happen to me. Currently, I have been awake for 35 minutes and it seems like everything seems misfortunate and miserable already. Alright, this is how I feel now, however there must be a reason. It just got to be a reason, I refuse not to think of a reason. It hits me. I am scared today. Utterly, secretively, genuinely scared. I am scared today. Today I am not fearless and I am surely not in a shape I would like to be. I feel disgraced and dishonoured and it makes it difficult for me to try this day out. It makes it feel impossible to go further with this and to go further with what is ahead of me this day. I am scared of myself changing and I am scared of myself being someone different. I am scared of letting go and I am scared of finding something else. I am scared of letting through my feelings and emotions and I am scared of showing them and sharing them to my family. I am scared I am not enough. I am scared of having the responsibility for myself. I am scared I do not have the strength to carry myself and to be my own saviour. I am scared of today. I am scared of tomorrow. I am scared.

19

To be waiting for something can seem to be a lasting infinite amount of time and days, hours, minutes and even seconds. I believe in the saying of "one who waits for something good never waits too long". Also, I do not, because what if that part of "good" was not really as you thought it would be. I have decided to see every opportunity, every possibility and chance to see something good in every step of the way I get through and I have decided that the grass is not greener on the other side, it is quite on the contrary. According to me, the one who waits for something "good" for a very long time, probably waits for nothing and probably you will be waiting for the same kind of days to come as the ones you are being present around right now. I also believe that truth and reality hurts and it hurts as hell. It hurts until you wonder for what reason exactly you are fighting this fight for. However, to me the answer was suddenly so simple, utterly easy and most importantly reachable for every human being thinking that the grass is greener or the other side. Deal with it. Fight with it not against it. Appreciate what you have and not what you could have had or could have reached or could have maintained, because guess what, it belongs to the past most of the times or is simply a deal of time wasting and people pleasing the wrong people, spending your time for granted. Thinking you are for granted and therefore come up with the idea that there is ALWAYS something better and always something waiting for you, every day, hoping for this day to come. However, I do not want to be the one who kills dreams, but the fact is I was myself one of the human beings always and always and always wished for something else, something better, something unreal even, as you have read earlier in this insane book, believing it so strongly I became mad, as you have already understood, probably. The fact is, no ones grass will get greener unless you water the grass and let it grow the way it is today. It will not look healthier, or greener or even grow at all if you do not look after it, and look after it carefully, every single day. Meaning, you own grass that you already have in front of you will get greener as soon as you see the beautiful characteristics and opportunities it carries; What is already there. The grass in front of you is your reality and is there for you, take care of it.

20

Travelling is a very wide range of experiences
and a very large amount of human beings
strolling around our world today spend a lot of
time travelling. They spend a lot of time in
existing cities, islands, countries and cultures
which may lead to please that sort of thirst
after seeing something else and seeing
something new, however this will ultimately be
something enjoyable for a couple of hours or
days for some people, however, when it comes
to always travelling, always being at new places
and most unfortunate all by yourself it will
start to confuse you, it will happen that nobody
will be at your hotel room and airbnb and be
waiting for you to come home with a freshly
made spaghetti carbonara. It will come to
mind that suddenly, among all of the existing
tourist attractions, cafes, restaurants and
famous parks or areas, you feel alone and you
feel like nobody cares for you or that nobody is
there for you because those parts you gave up
long ago when starting to always be on a
wandering foot, place after place, country after
country which will be dangerous and seriously
harmful for you mind, body, spirit and soul

and eventually your very heart as it stops beating for you, never being loved by yourself or anyone else anymore. All that is beating is frozen margaritas by yourself at a New York City bar and taxis taking you to all kinds of places. All because you are thinking there are no reasons for you reality to keep going. To keep fighting. Fighting for what? First class tickets and grand hotel hotel rooms with a glass of chardonnay included every three hours of being present among that god damn hotel? Is it worth giving up family, hobbies, relationships, your life long journey of hours by suffocating yourself to work and simply miss out on every possible, existing opportunity and ability to feel instead, to feel and experience ultimate presence and the feeling of you being so utterly enough you do not have to proof absolutely anything. If you keep running away it most likely mean you feel like you have to proof to your boss, parents, friends or colleagues if you are hard working enough, or healthy enough or taking enough pictures from your trips. Those actions are a hideous waste of time and even more miserable memories will arrive if keep going with this kind of lifestyle. However, there is a kind of travelling which according to me have opened up a whole new world of perspectives, knowledge and comfort for my soul and heart to be able to experience such inspiring stories and personal journeys and very high valued stories in our history travelling me to places which I have never been able to see before. Travelling with books, travelling through books. My next destination is a new book, the next book to arrive to. I add it to my routine, my everyday routine. Reading makes me travel, travel through events and history and journals and stories and it helps me learn through words and the expressions from those words which sticks in my head for days and months and hopefully for every year to come. It is existential in such dazzling mindful way there is no such greater thing. Reading is travelling and it is travelling through time, spirits, memories, experiences, cultures, ways and trips you have never been experiencing before. Wisdom comes from reading that includes wisdom itself in the very book and all you need to do is simply open that book and read. Read for as many hours as you would have spent in Rome, or Paris or Bali or wherever it would be, and it costs you very much less money than a flight ticket. To escape through vacations only, trips and weekend trips only is to escape from yourself and your everyday life. You probably already know it and that is an even bigger issue and harder problem to deal with to not face the fact, your own truth and reality. Therefore,

instead of escaping, make sure to gather all
your strength, your guts and then you face it
with dignity and maturity and find your
solution to escaping; reading.

21

Movement, simplicity, our feet. Movement. Simplicity. Our feet. We maintain movement by moving our feet and we maintain movement by moving our body and by simply stepping forward one foot after another. The morning is astonishing and so is walking during the morning until noon. Before car hunks and chatter among the streets. Before even the natural world has woken up, birds, the rise of the sun, the wind being present among trees and leaves. Before people start to walk on the street with cell phones, yelling at their boss or their kid, before people have had their coffee for the reason to be inhumanly active and awake in a way you start wondering if they are going crazy. Which they probably are since that type of energy is almost scary to someone who tries to take in every moment with breathing, our eyes and our feet. And those elements only. When walking I put my phone away. I even leave any sort of belongings at home every single time to make sure I am vividly present and wholly in no sense of control or planning or even having the thought of even knowing where I am going. I am simply putting my feet in front of another one step at a time watching them move, watching the atmosphere become alive as I walk, how everything starts to move yet everything is so still it is ridiculous. I pass the empty stores, and then maybe one alive person rushing for their 4 am work beginning at 6 am at a cafe probably. I pass empty park benches, empty entrances to the subway where all I can really hear and sense are the empty subways passing by in that very ugly tunnel. I pass by empty cafes, restaurants and the noises in my head is only the noises I hear within my head. I walk around thinking about and therefore hearing words and sentences and emotions popping up because I let them. I hear them appear in such way: "how marvellous this fresh air feels", "my feet feels very light today", "what about this cafe, maybe I should try it, or maybe it will be very expensive, who knows, lets see later in the day". And then something like, "hey you beautiful son of a bird, the hell are you doing up so early?", and the conversation with my head and myself goes on and it feels truly prodigious to be awake this day, this time, this moment, to be present among this moment. Because it is not only a part of my day, it is THE part of the day and it is definitely the most important part of my day to be alone, present and very aware of the fact that even if walking alone among these empty streets, I will never feel lonely because the stores and the birds, sun, the wind and the cleaning cars being on the streets every morning are with me and I am not alone. I am alone but I am not feeling lonely and that is something very precious and a very magnificent feeling of presence. Simplicity is beautiful and so is walking. Walking is simple, simple is beautiful and what is beautiful comes from simplicity, essentials, not more not less. Simplicity.

22

Cleansing and vanishing, restarting and creating patterns, routines, habits and adding necessary parts to your day to fully relax, be quiet and to be able to feel enough during your day. As I walked and moved my body second thing in the morning after a burning hot shower and putting on everything but high fashionable, women like clothes, therefore something called utterly comfortable and body friendly clothes, not too tight, not too loose but fitting and something that simply makes me feel ready to be seen, heard and touched with whatever words my family, a stranger or a co worker will say to me today. If the words come with love I will feel warmth and the desire to be loving back, if it comes from stress and anger, frustration and a person who experienced a total lack of sleep last night, I will be able to bounce it off and fully ignore the fact that those words came directly "to me" when in reality, in my mind and her or his mind, it was directly to themselves and they sure know it too. As I walked and moved my body this morning I was then afterwards prepared for precisely everything to be coming

towards me or not coming towards me this
very day after this very morning. I am ready
for whatever the world has to offer me and this
is plainly thanks to my choice of routine,
innately puts me in this mental shield of safety
and strength, awareness and protection which
makes me feel like the very much most humble
person I could have ever experienced during
the day. The morning. Very crucial yet utterly
fateful which makes it my most respectful part
of the day and the most crucial for the other
parts of my day to arrive and when those parts
of the day arrives I will be standing with
gratitude and calmness facing whatever have to
be or wants to be faced, by my choice or not by
my choice, to meet the obstacle, the
opportunity, kindness or evilness with the same
state of mind no matter what kind of message
is sends me or the whole wide world for that
matter. I will meet it with force of stillness and
force of kindness because that is how my day
started and that will be for the rest of the day,
not for you, not for them and certainly not for
anyone else but me. It makes me feel needed
for my own day and it makes me feel like the
only choice I have that is to keep going and
keep being, not faint but being, and in the most
desirable way I wish to achieve a meaning
from my day. And because of doing it the most
desirable way for me, I automatically and

naturally create a more sensible and accurate, loving atmosphere and surrounding around everybody else, being able to give a helping hand and have patience with them. I will have the energy and strength to do so, showing love for myself first and then for the people around me. For me it is an obvious gesture, obvious act of my own nature, helping others, taking care of others, strangers or relatives, to also at the very end of the day being able to think and feel and appear as a loving person wanting to help not only myself but others as well. I believe we were born with other people for a reason and a reason to believe we are about to evolve and develop with these people as well, to develop with them, not against them, not having a competition about anything, rather just be and grow together which is the biggest source and power of love. People coming together, showing that they care, expressing through tranquility and peace, serenity and silence to let the very deepest, most important, most human benignly emotions and words come through words and letters, not through violence and abrupt, impulsive choices making you regret and fear. Making you become scared and uncomfortable with the world rather than letting your soul align with it and letting your mind cooperate with it, letting your heart be seen and experienced by what or who wants to get to know your heart and your true desires and hopes, wishes and beliefs. Let your routine build your strength and let the rest of your routine during the rest of the day be the most important part of your day so that you will be able to act with love and kindness, and to have the ability to face whatever is in front of you this very day, not in a year, not in two days, but today. Only today.

23

Adjustments and difference can be difficult and quite overwhelming not only for the person choosing to make adjustments, like me and many people out there, or trying to be different but I have acknowledged and noticed how much it affects my surroundings and environment around family and friends. This is something fully comprehensible to me that it can be shocking to people and even jealousy, fear and and a sort of dislike can appear which should be fully treated with respect and patience from my side, however it is hard for me as well to really describe or explain, to make them understand how much it means to me and at the same time I have no need to explain or describe because it is simply a process, simply a happening within my life that yes they are a part of but no I do not need to feel an obligation to feel needed to or even worse, a must to explain myself in any case. However, I want to relate and to accept me for my choice of change but it is utterly important to me that no matter what my environment think of me and choose to observe and recognise me I will always continue with my chosen, desirable pathway that brings me joy everyday and that brings me a feeling of being whole and enough, because we are, and a state of mind which brings me unity with myself and it brings me down to earth. The point is, do not let anyone, not even a sibling or your closest friend let you think any differently, because that sort of neglect and underestimating comes from their insecurity and has nothing to do with you. Also, if someone in your nearest and dearest environment, when it comes to friendship and relationship ever treats you this way, let it go and let it be, do not let it come near you. Ever. We have no time to waste time and we have no time to let others, not even yourself, let you feel those things when it takes a lot of effort, time, energy and self confidence to even make the choice to follow yourself and to follow what brings you serenity. To make a change. Because that is just it, it is not only words or a comment or a reaction from somebody, because those words, letters, comments and reactions goes right into our mind and head and we start thinking, interpreting and if you are a truly emotional person, which by the way are our bravest people among this world, it will be hard to process and hard to think in another way for that moment. We did not come this far to let this come in to our mind, but we did come this far to choose who we spend time with and we came this far to choose what we let our minds soak in and what to simply leave outside our brain. We choose everything. Nobody chooses for us. Choices are the path to difference and change, let it be something worthy and powerful, not something that frightens us and therefore to start with, really think about your environment today. Who do you let in? What people of you communicate with? How much time do you spend with those you actually care about? What brings you your highest high during the day? And also very important and crucial, what brings your lowest low? Think about it and notice what feelings comes up when thinking about it and notice what brings you a feeling of safety and love and what brings you a feeling of anguish and heartache. Really, carefully think about it.

24

I stare out through the window when I wake
up, before I shower in the morning, the second
I walk out the door, when having breakfast,
when reading afterwards, when having lunch
and when reading again afterwards and then
before I go out for a walk again after lunch and
then when having dinner and before going to
sleep sitting at the table for the last time and
when brushing my teeth in the bathroom. As I
lay in bed right before the lights go out I stare
out the window and acknowledged the detailed
elements, the last pieces of leaves before I
decide to gently close my eyes and having the
very strong thought in my mind of desire for
sleep as this moment and the desire and
knowledge of me being well rested for what is
yet to arrive during the day that is slowly
arriving. I stare out the window to make me
feel a part of something and I stare out the
window whenever I feel disconnected in some
sort of way, I stare out the window which
makes me feel safe and calm, hearing noises
from the outside very slightly and very lightly,
yet noticeable and the thought of the world
moving outside is fully diverting and

entertaining and it is almost even more enough than actually stepping outside into it and to be a part of it. However, I love the balance between these two sort of connections between being outside with everything and everyone, being a part of what is going on around me is a truly marvellous feeling and to be a part of something I sometimes do not comprehend and understand how it even works or why some things looks the way they do, the principles, design, functions of things, however that is the inspiring part because I enjoy to not know everything and surely like to come up with my own ideas of something making it to my own object with its own meaning and function. The important part is that I am being able to step outside and see these very details and objects around me just being making me just want to be and be there with it or with her or him. I love the balance between feeling the movement in the very specific moment being out in the streets and also sitting inside seeing what is going on and hearing sounds of people, engines, traffic, cafes and restaurants which as much as the moment being on the streets among all of it makes me feel like I am present among these happenings even sitting at the window. To be a part of something else than myself, something else than anyone else is a very harmonising state of mind where you can just put yourself not needing or have the must to do anything really. Just look at everything, sense everything, smell everything, feel everything, touch everything, seize everything, interpret everything. What is going on? Not, what is happening here, but what is truly going on? Is there people around and what are they doing? The trees, do they move, is it windy outside, does the leaves fall on the ground? Is it fall? Is it summer, spring or winter? What is happening around you and how do you feel about it? I love balance. I also love strolling on the streets having no plan, destination, time reference, limits or must or needs. I am just being and I am being by strolling, strolling around and sensing every single happening, feeling, emotion, reaction. Simply everything. I love every part of it and I love it som much it makes me feel so alive it is almost insane. Suddenly I am so present it is beyond words to describe and beyond comprehension if you do not get out there and try it out. The recipe follows, use your mind, body and eyes. Your mind to sense, your body to move and get to another street, your eyes to feel with, to sense with, to acknowledge. With this method you will be able to feel what presence is about and what wonderful, glorifying ability we humans carry everyday to

be able to be present and see the grace our
world includes.

25

Black and white. Nothing at all or all in.
Contrasts. The feeling of wether only eating
that or only eating this. The demand for utter
control or utter absence. The must of either
always having the feeling or needing to do
something or never have the feeling of needing
something or needing to do something. To go
all in and party all the time or to not go all in
and party all night and all the time. To not eat
anything at all or to order McDonalds every
single night. To have this sort of thinking is
imbalance and disorganisation, disorientation
which leads us to the very fundamental,
accusing mental, physical, chronicle diseases
among every human being today which among
even "healthy" considered people (to
themselves according to some site on how to
loose three pounds during a day) with
"healthy" habits even them have this sort of
thinking sometimes which may work or seem
meaningful and they may believe it works for a
week, telling everyone how beautiful and
fantastic they feel where at the same time that
is not the truth at all and it is not to be
followed since their reality is jacked up among

the utter feeling or being either this or that and
if they are not either this or that they are not
enough and they must stick to this way of
being because otherwise they have no value,
and no sense of humanity among themselves.
Listen to this. How ugly ones life can be. To be
living so strictly or too loose and live out of
control with no sense of limits or routine, not
even a routine on how to get out of bed. I will
tell you that I have been within this state of
mind and yes, I used to think it was about
either never sleeping and being out until 6 am
and them go to work at a cafe at 7 and I used
to really believe this is the way to live, never
having time or energy or love for my family
and friends who actually cares about me and
whom I actually care about too, not my selfish,
disgusting, middle aged, fat boss. I used to also
believe when I was 14 that eating only greens,
no milk, no sugar, no gluten, no sweets of any
sorts, not even fruits at som times would make
be the most powerful woman on earth and
would also help me with my skin and loose
weight which it did actually, in a very
miserable, quite dangerous and life depending
way I ended up at the emergency section in the
hospital being told to not leave until I have had
something to eat if that was even a crumble
from a berry. I used to believe in seeing, and
eating and appearing as black or white, this or

that, this way or no way as if I were never enough and as if what I already had and had so very much to be thankful for was not enough I sure was not enough to even be alive or breathing. I was blind. Blind to everything and everyone and for that I am sorry for myself but at the same time it is called a journey and this is the crucial part of life where opportunities and choices appears everywhere, all the time, among everyone, among every period of time and parts of our days which gives you the holy responsibility to reflect about and so I did, I started to learn about balance, I learned about self awareness and self-respect. I learned about the very fundamental life changing element called enough, which have been my best buddy to this very day and will be for the rest of my breathing lungs journey on this spinning son of a sphere until I will not be present among this son of a spinning sphere anymore. To live by extreme limits or severe, too much of unlimited standards will give you unnecessary choices, responsibility and will take away the important in life, family and hobbies. Enough is enough. Enough is balance. Being enough is the way to be. Believe that you are enough and your whole perspective on life will sooner or later lead you to the belief that all you have,

everything you have worked for is enough and
no need for more. More is sickness.

26

I believe there are different ways of being present and I believe there are different sorts of presence and attendance among us which can either be mental or external. Why is it that the outside seem to matter that much? Why is it that clothes and shoes and scarfs and handbags and leather goods all of a sudden decided to be the most important part of presence and why is it that either a pair of jeans or a pair of joggers makes us appear casual or formal? Why is it that the external world seems to decide who we are, what we do and therefore how we should act and think and observe and and behave, all because of a watch or a whole in someone pants. I believe I have seen and heard enough and I believe the world should really consider this as a massive problem, an issue to not only themselves but for the future and what it has to offer. Of course it matters in our present the most, but our present leads us somewhere, does it not? To be valued by what we wear, what we own, what we do not own and what we look like, the external world of presence which has no meaning but fraud and dishonesty. It is by far

the ugliest part of us and the ugliest part of
our society to be measured by and recognised
by and valued by what we own and then be a
fool to call it presence in a sense that
everything that matters is how we appear and
look. How we appear and look externally and
subjectively, not mentally. The mental is the
flower flourishing and thriving inside us
wanting to be seen and heard, respected and
loved. The mental drives us forward, it helps us
create this so called personality, the mental is
our existence and the mental is presence.
Presence is all about where our head is, where
our thoughts are placed, where our emotions
takes place, where reactions, interpretations,
experiences, memories, our knowledge, human
being fundamentals takes place and it makes us
a living, thinking organism that thanks to
mental presence makes us a person who are
able to sense and feel all of this. Our mentality
is our presence. External presence do exist,
and it exists because people existing this way
has no mentality and no source of tranquility
or humility and therefore greatness can not
take place and when the mind can not take
place in our bodies then the system will
corrupt and you will feel as you appear as an 9
am - 12 pm robot, senseless, emotionless,
hopeless, being built up by arrogance, your ego
and junk food which leads you to the most non

present organism walking around on this earth. No matter the numbers on your bank account, no matter if your jacket is from Walmart or Gucci, no matter what a "gorgeous" bimbo to a wife you have. It does not matter at all because all you are being "present" among are these materials which leads you nowhere but to a black hole full of misery, in some cases drugs, alcohol and disbelief around yourself and everything you built up. It starts making no sense, because you yourself do not make sense and then you will realize, what am I working for? For who? For what? For me? Why? Some numbers on my bank account? What for? A trip to Bahamas? Then what? You will start to feel this utter loneliness even when you feel like you are around everything and when you can touch and see and experience whatever you want. Then what? Jump from a plane? Then what? What else is there to do with that money? Take an overdose? Then what? Oh right, you are already gone. This I the thing with external, objective, materialistic presence, you find no worth, value, love or calm in your life and so wherever you go all you can show up with is your new pair of shoes or a new jacket. But guess what? Nobody cares and nobody ever will and the only one making this misery is the ego, you itself and once believing in external presence you will sense a ridiculous feeling of not being enough. Every. Single. Day. Because enough is never enough for you and you always want more and more and more until there is nothing left but yourself in the graveyard with no one visiting you because what should you be remembered for? The Tesla in your garage or the 300 million dollar knife in your kitchen which by the way you do not even use, admit it, cause you order in all the time, Chinese food or some shit. External presence means the end, and a very close end. Think about the way you appear. Is it externally or mentally? Is it with your precious mind and the knowledge of love, respect and tranquility it includes? Or is it externally, by the way you dress and what you own? Really think and then think again and again, until you end up with the answer that you are enough and materialistic things is not a part of you, it is not a part of anyone. We came here without it, lets not pretend it suddenly is all we have to live by.

27

To be able to find peace and serenity, quiet and calm within the chaos, among the cars, around people, around sounds, around traffic and bars and restaurants and coffee shops. Whenever you go there, whenever we go there, it is a sort of noise of rumbling and shouting, laughing, crying and maybe someone is having an intense argument. Even worse if one of them has a little alcohol in their blood at that very moment. How is it even possible to find silence and calmness around all this? How could we ever be able to handle all of these noises without feeling jacked up, overwhelmed, discouraged, disorganised and stressed? There are reasons for the social anxiety being among us today. There are reasons for stress to occur among us today and there is certainly a reason for us to start handle it with care and to handle it in a way you will be able to feel utterly comfortable among all of these situations no matter what country you are in with their culture, no matter if it is at your favourite coffee shop or if you have an issue with the subway. The real solution within chaos is to face it but not only to face it but facing it with stillness. To face everything with a double perspective eye and a sense of tranquility, knowing yourself so well no one could ever make you feel like you are not supposed to be where you are standing right now, or that you yourself limit yourself from finding peace in chaotic moments. However, to constantly and maybe "living" at these places, always going out, always being at coffee shops, always having dinner with "friends", and never have the time to be alone, then that is probably the most important part of this "not being able to handle chaos" situation, just because you do not even know what silence means, what stillness means, why being able to find calmness among these situations even matter and why some people are amusingly good at it and why some people always seem to think life and death in every single minimum sort of situation because it involves the slightest amount of stress, overwhelm or fear. To be scared is to not have a solution for your fear. To be scared is a sign that your body is trying to tell you, less of this more of that. To be scared is your body telling you to stop, is this really how I want to feel facing obstacles? Is this really the energy I want to carry among slightest problems or issues? Is this really scary? Most of the times it is not. And most of the time that sort of fear comes from a wound or scar, a traumatic experience or memory. It is most likely your inner child voice speaking to you, saying, "hey I am scared, can we not approach this or do this or that?" This is the part where it is the very right and appropriate time to do the opposite of what your inner child voice is telling you by simply going ahead, face your fears and challenge yourself. How else do you solve being scared of something? To just sit there and do nothing? I fit only were that easy, but guess what it is really not and it is not supposed to be easy, at all. I am thinking you already know this as well. It requires patience, belief and discipline. It requires a "one day at a time" sort of schedule with consistency and the clear thinking of always believing in what you are doing and believing that the goal is not the end, keep developing even after achieving what you have achieved and keep exploring, try out new things, keep exploring within yourself and you yourself ahead. Keep exploring with your thoughts. Why am I thinking this or that way? Why did this come to mind at this very moment? Why is this feeling so very very strong this morning and how can I appreciate it or the opposite, say no, this feeling belongs to someone else or something else. Keep focusing on your path and not others and keep helping those you want to help and not the ones you feel obligated or a must to be helping because that takes your energy and it takes away your ability to grow and it takes away your opportunity to face your fears because then, when giving all your energy to everybody else there is nothing else left for you and your own issues and so they stay in a shape they have always been and will always be. It is simply time to prioritise, remove what is already gone and should not be in use, both materialistic and when it comes to relationships, situations. It is also time to reflect and then not wasting time on whatever makes you avoid your insecurities and your fears because they will never ever go away unless you put action to it and show it some love instead of avoiding it. Become a friend with your fears and insecurities, treat it like you would treat someone you really care about and treat for as long as it is needed for the wound to heel. Spend time on seeing the truth and act with patience and calmness to your fears and they will disappear, slowly, but remember slow is fast and slow is the way to go.

28

There is no such thing as boredom, no such thing as pointless days unless you are spending them in a complete boring and pointless way. There is no such thing as this or that is because of this or that for no reason. There is no growth in always blaming everything else, everyone else and simply everything existing for your own boredom or pointless day. To sense the arising day as pointless or boring it is simply because your daily tasks or schedule, your agenda and "to do list" simply looks like crap and of course it will feel like crap. If you always have something on your agenda, does not matter if it is something exciting and something that you look forward to or again, if it is something boring or pointless, according to you. The point is if you always have something to do, to always have your schedule filled up and planned, controlled, prepared for every single day, even weekends for som people it will make your days pretty (fucking) boring and it will make them pretty damn pointless since all you seem to do is doing, doing and doing. Where there is no time for being, being, being with the freedom of not watching the clock, not in a rush for a meeting or a date, not anxious about if you are getting a raise or not at the office which you by the way despise, truly hate, even your colleagues, but hey you are doing it for the check right?, You are doing it for the money, nothing else and so it seems to be so utterly important to you. In fact your schedule with returning stuff, attending to meetings, going on stupid dates takes up all of your time, and then suddenly that is what your life is about and what your life will be about if your calendar will forever be this way. The marvellous thing is, there is a change possible and I believe your body is truly waiting for it to be present among you since right now you are naturally, slowly and quietly killing yourself softly and gently and therefore everything seems boring and pointless. It seems boring and pointless because you have no time for the inner experience and the inner value. It seems boring and pointless because you have no time for your family, appointments that actually do matter and maybe you have kids but there is no time for them because the donna in the bar is more important than your 5 year old daughter needing her fathers love and time. Right now, you are most likely to not listen to yourself at all and is therefore avoiding the fact that your inner voice is trying to help you and say something to you but you choose not to listen and to interpret it as something unnecessary and annoying. Something boring and pointless. Well, at this point it is almost impossible to think in another way since your mindset and head and all your inner self beliefs and emotions and feelings and thoughts is about your pointless and boring schedule. To have a pointless and boring schedule means that you also can not give your true self to either you or anyone else and for that reason when not being able to be true to yourself and to express what you really care about and live for, people around you will also find you disorganised and feel your pointless and boring schedule through their bodies and minds which leads you to find people apart from your loving family to instead start relationship with the similar minded, pointless and boring people who also have these kind of thoughts of their days, pointless and boring. You will find these kind of people as and connect with them even though that may not even be the human beings you prefer to be around or even prefer seeing or knowing or talking about, even hear about. But here you are around these people because they matches your energy and your way of thinking, your spirit and everyday life schedule, pointless and boring which automatically drags you there and to those minds thinking the same way you think at this point. The inspirational, self confidence, still, present and mindful people are yet to be out there and are yet for you to get to know you and for you to get to know them, to help and support and show you love, and for you to do the same to them, however there is no way possible if you are not ready to let go of the unnecessary and give space to the fundamentals parts of a humans life to feel utter meaning and to feel supported by the world not against it. The world is not your enemy, you are. Another way of having a pointless or boring life includes the feeling of always trying to prove someone something, to prove someone your life is not pointless or boring, to prove that you do own a value, to prove that you are enough and that you have a schedule like a "professional", that you have friends who can get you in at the most popular places in town, bars, cafes, clubs etc etc etc. Boring and pointless. Pointless and boring. It will forever stick within your journey if reflection, truth and stillness will not have a place in your everyday schedule. Redo your calendar, erase the most unnecessary, wether if it is a meeting, for you to get a raise or if it is about a tinder date which will probably most likely end up in the category of adding more pointlessness and boredom into your schedule than valued plans. Let me ask you, when did

you last time spend time with yourself?
Walking the streets by yourself? Playing some
cards, sit by the window and reflect, make
yourself some tea and feel utter stillness
around you? When did you last take time to
just be? At these moments you will feel
fulfilment, a sense of really starting to make
time for yourself, a sense of taking care of
yourself and your very own intelligent mind
with the strength of being able to neglect, say
no, with grace but with strength. You will have
the strength to always know, wether you did
not or did attend to that date that you are
enough and enough is, again, the most
appreciative quality a human being can own
and be confident about. Certainly the part of
being confident within this part of you is by far
the most important part and will decide wether
you believe it or not, because by simply saying
that you are enough does not mean anything, it
is by actions and by being honest and true to
yourself that you can start seeing yourself as
enough and naturally, automatically people
around you will sense that sort of feeling of
you being enough. This means a less pointless
and boring life with instead will lead you to
beautiful intentions, a purpose and another
way of being; present.

29

We do have eyes for a reason, right? And we did achieve them by the universe for us to be able to examine and observe, to watch things and to witness whatever is happening around us. However, I do not believe we were given these beautiful narrow binoculars, namely our eyes to judge, scan people or gaze at them as if they were a piece of garbage. I do not believe people are meant to stare or look at other people with repulsion and impoliteness with a sense of anger or disgust, because that is simply ugly and selfish and without doubt truly unnecessary. I believe this is called jealousy and it is an act of enviousness which human beings certainly seem to love and to really appreciate for some reason. To feel jealous and to envy other people for what they have or for what they wear, for what they look like, for what they own. More interestingly the envy ends up being presented and existing through acts of disrespect and offensiveness. Imagine blind people. As all of us we were given this beautiful part of our body which is our eyes to be able to recognise their loved ones, to be able to see miracles and places which you have

never seen before, to be able to see the world's
sunset and sunrise every morning, to be able to
see the first snow, the leaves falling from the
trees while sitting on a park bench. To be able
to see. Yet, for us who are able to use our eyes
and are able to see and acknowledge, misuse
this ability for certain and more or less
underestimating the astonishing possibilities it
gives us. However, instead we use it to frighten
people, to simply look at one as if they had no
value at all when all you can do is keep your
jealousy to yourself and your teammates who
are also being jealous as hell and envy
everything and everyone and keep going with
that energy, but do not let anyone else get
affected and do not let yourself poison other
souls trying to develop into something so much
more valuable and cheerful than envy and
jealousy. What others have and how other look
like do not matter to human beings being
settled, having prioritised what matters, a
stable routine, a mental strength telling you
everyday you are enough and I need nothing
else than what I have and the only search for
something greater is within me, to travel within
ourselves beyond limits that makes our souls
rich, and our heads full of knowledge and our
legs filled with muscles from the many walks
and strolls we have been through during
everyday and everyday to come. Let our minds

be fed by awakening visions and beautiful souls
who are there to help and let our minds be
creative and free and let our bodies achieve the
greatness it deserves through meaningful walks
and conversations boosting our whole system
to the point where there will never, even if our
life depended on it, be one single feeling or
emotion or act of envy or jealousy. Acts of
envy and jealousy is a sign of true insecurity
you carry. To put simply, if your day is about
gossiping, nagging, grumbling and
complaining and the worst part, if all of this
crap is pointed towards something or someone
else rather than yourself, it means you have a
bunch of responsibility and obligation to take
care of which is clearly missing from the first
place. It means to take care of your wounds, to
take care of your priorities and choices you
make, because they certainly are not the right
choices for you and certainly are not the right
reasons for your own world to look the slightest
safe and comfortable. It means it is time for a
change and also it is time to open your eyes,
because they do not sound like they are open
to me if this behaviour is completely normal to
you and certainly not healthy, not among the
present and not for the long run either.. How
can one human being want to live among
resentment which ends up in dishonesty and
disvalued days when there is so much more to

be experienced and explored in our world. Open your eyes, see what you already have and see what your environment already have offered you because only then you will understand what your true belongings really are, your loved ones, hopefully food for the day and eyes to be opened whenever you want them to be open and then be able to see our world with eyes of perspective and eyes of respect and humility. Eyes are a gift. Let's treat them as a gift and not something we should take for granted.

30

Seasons and periods of time where everything looks and feel different and changes all the time. From heated streets thanks to our sunlight hitting us during the day, almost at night as well, to cold and dark yet peaceful winters with the ability to have time to reflect and rest. We have seasons in between as well where spring and autumn arrives and they tend to arrive when we least expect it every single time. Just as our seasons change, we should change, in shapes and forms, colours and characteristics. We should change the way the rain falls down and then all of a sudden the sun rises and everybody gets outside. We should change like the seasons because we are a part of these seasons and I believe the nature is meant to change and develop, as are we humans supposed to change and develop because what else is there to focus on and what else is there to admire rather than change? Our world is constantly in construction to reach new levels of diversity and adjustments to make our world a better place for all of us. Our world is also meant to be in this sort of way for it to be alive, because without change and development how would we ever even be present among our earth, how would we even survive the way we are able to survive today without development and change, knowledge and help and support from the people around us. We have doctors, scientists, writers and painters for a reason and that reason is our world changing and developing every day from. Therefore, change is not just change, it is a pathway to civilisation, humanity to make our lives alive and to make our days full of life and for us to be a part of the everyday change and development going on is also necessary to feel like you are a part of the society and not a part of the idle world where nothing ever moves or continues, takes care of or even being noticed. It is important to be a apart of this sort of movement to be able to feel the life in a society, to be able to continue with yourself and what you desire to fulfil during your day, meaning you take care of yourself and change in a way that feels comfortable to you but at the same time in a way that feels new and exciting for that that to be possible you need something, action for the most part, to help you wanting to change. It is not for the feeling of being better or more or to feel some sort of power over other people because of change, it is for you and only for you to travel within yourself and what you are really able to do when it comes to that personal journey and where it can take you by exploring and experiencing and choosing the excitement and desires before "what you should do" and what "you think would be good", and "what other people tell you to do" and not for yourself. Sometimes we think of change as something for someone else, and yes that could be the case for a specific goal or reason that is very meaningful to both of you. However when it comes to your personal journey and your individual inner self process and development, nobody else but you can be within this picture. It is a risk and it is irrelevant for your change to happen. Dare to believe in change and dare to do it by yourself and for yourself as a priority. Also, dare to reach out for inspiration and similar minded people for their support and guidance when you feel like you really need advice and help in any sort of way. To ask for help, to inspire from other peoples stories and developing journeys means strength and curiosity, it means to learn and teach and it is utterly loving and supporting. Change and development is also something to be founded and presented among silence, among stillness, among the quietness around us. At this part you might also think that it is ridiculous since we are very rarely ever able to find silence among these days. It usually goes like; I have three kids, 9-5 job and at the evening I really enjoy going out with the girls, or no way I love gaming and the sound of killing all day long and then during nights I work at McDonald's making some fries so that I can pay for the games I buy and so I can feel totally miserable for just another day, and then another one and another one and another one and so it goes on. Excuses and avoidance are one of the ugliest forms of acting we human beings are able to choose from when it comes to dare to break a routine and to change something. Think about it, walking around in the city, or at your job, at school, at restaurants, in the subway, at home or wherever you are there are buzzing, and noises, people making noises, cars making noises, teachers yelling, the school cafeteria at lunch time being slaughtered by voices and actions, the subway during after work hours looking like a zoo etc etc etc. On top of it we found that there must be something else, another noise we add to our minds during these situations, music, podcasts, movies, series etc etc etc. Before going to bed we listen to sounds which could be calm ones, still they are sounds. During night we hear car hunks and ambulances or someone screaming outside our window, probably a drunk dork. When will there be silence? During exactly what moment during your day do you experience utter silence? We are scared of silence. Silence is therapy, medicine, recovery and truly significant and crucial, for your mind, body, spirit, for your wellness and for you to even be able to exist without always feeling tired, always feeling like you or the world is not plenty enough, always feeling like whatever is coming up or whatever the day has to offer makes you feel stressed and exhausted and then always feeling like you want to stay in bed, watch movies all day long, eat burgers and fries, milkshakes and brownies, donuts and then some more fries because you pity yourself so much and feel bad for yourself. For what reason? No one else but you choose whatever you chose and no one else but you choose to not change the way you live. For what reason? It does not matter where you are present right now and for what reason you are alive rather than you deserve to be here and you deserve the very best for yourself and therefore your loved ones. It does not matter what you do for living or how you live, you still always walk around with choices that has the power to change and that change could be a new season of your life, a new period with new colours, shapes, forms and thoughts which can lead you to feel like you are a part of the society, not against it and against the people among our society. Similar and loving minded people are there to support and inspire. There are also people who are willing to do the opposite and those we simply ignore and handle with care to protect our inner selfs. Even if that is your sister or a stranger. Believe in change as our seasons change and let the change come to you and let yourself then choose to allow it in your life, starting from today. Change is the key to a valuable reality.

31

I am addicted to walking. Addicted to the feeling of it, the thought of it, the present experience of it. Everything. I am addicted to walking and for that I am grateful. Walking in the early morning, which is a part of my routine, walking for hours and hours, processing, thinking, making my mind empty and with a feeling that I have no control and no clue, I simply just walk and have no demands from either myself or anyone else among me, no musts or needs, just walking. I walk until my legs are numb and my head is empty and until my heart feels relieved and full of new love and energy from that movement and fresh air. I am addicted to walking and it may sound insane but is it by far the very most important, meaningful and valuable part of my day, every day that I walk as much as almost 5 hours a day. There is something with walking that generates my processing. Processing and figuring out whatever needs to be figured out, wether it is a decision I want to make, wether it is about a relationship or a family situation. However, the very most important and crucial reason me walking is because everything starts with my walks and everything ends with my walks. It is crucial because otherwise I would not be able to write, to be who I am today, to feel the way I do, to have the routine I have today, to even sense meaning with anything at all. Because walking puts my whole self into ease and it makes me feel so empty that I feel full of calmness and appreciation, lust and motivation for whatever I want to do or for whatever I desire to develop and process etc etc etc. When walking I come up with ideas for my writing, I solve any problems being present within my head and within my life that are very meaningful to me and so I want to solve them. When walking everything starts to make sense and I believe it brings me such comfort and relaxation that all of a sudden I notice everything and it is not just a walk anymore. I am able to help one in need, to let the mum with her baby walk before me crossing the street, to thank the motorist for slowing down just for me to be able to cross the street, to smile to a stranger, to hold the door for someone, to feel connected to people without even talking to them or touching them or even staring at them, non of that, just through kind gestures and daily habits when on my walks that are truly worthwhile and significant for me. Walking is to take care of myself, and should be to take care of yourself as well, but also it automatically takes care of others since it makes you process issues and those issues you have with your loved ones, it makes you see more clearly and helps you understand the issue better and gives you clarity to all that you are wondering about and to all questions you might or may have. It will give you answers and it will bring you a sense of utter tranquility because it will make your body feel exhausted, in a good way, because our legs are engines and we are supposed to use them as engines and to walk and walk and walk until every question is answered and until every piece of worry or anxiousness going on in that head of yours disappear and get processed making you feel relieved and lighter and instead full of stillness and peace that brings the ability for you to focus on your day without always having something in the way. Remember what we said about always having a full calendar, it leads you nowhere near solving issues you have and carry every day, so say "fuck off" to that meeting and let's go for a walk.

It is true that the ego is the enemy, and so it is time to cooperate with this "enemy" and make it your best friend, instead. Communicate with yourself, communicate what you feel and what you think of whatever you are dealing with or trying to handle or change, let your ego be aware of this and let your ego not be in the way for you because what you need is your soul to show, what really encourages you to be you and what really makes you, you. The ego however, must be lowered and not prioritised for you to be able to open up to something else and to see the other side of everything around you. Feel your legs move and you will see how everything else starts to move and you will also feel how your body starts to thank you by answering your questions. Let your body be rich in movement so that your heart will as well and so your head will function in a way it will help you and not be against you. With that being said; let's go for a walk.

32

Put your damn phone away. Put you damn phone away when you are having a conversation. Put your damn phone away when you are around your family and your loved ones, when having dinner, lunch, breakfast and any sort of meal at all. Put your damn phone away because there is absolutely no point in using it around these occasions and even more importantly, put your damn phone away when being outside, walking or running or just being outside, because what is there for you to look at is right in front of you, which should be the surrounding and the very bare environment itself, whoever you are with or if you are alone, put your damn phone away. There is something about today's society which tells us to always check our email, because 95% of our existing societies today owns a smartphone where you have everything, and when I say everything I mean EVERYTHING in our phone, from the amount of steps we take, to personal files and emails that "your life is depending on". "My phone is my life", "I have my whole life in this little shit", "Everything that matters to me is to be found within my phone". Bullshit. I say bullshit. Because life is what you have right in front of you. Life is reality, the bare, naked, challenging, beautiful, tough yet marvellous elements, not your phone. What you have in your phone, pictures, apps, camera, social media, those are the things that will bring you nothing near life. Those are the parts that has absolutely no value and the only function it has is to take up your worthwhile time with the purpose of making money and this is the wholly truth, companies creating apps, phones and digital gadgets to earn money. They spend hours and hours, years and days being miserable of the lack of sleep they get to make you loose valuable family time and valuable time for you to be able to only focus on the important things such as being present when having dinner once in a month with your mum, when having a conversation that means something to both of you etc. People likes to manipulate other people and certainly in todays companies, where it is all about money and will sadly always be as long as we keep dealing and behaving the way we do today. However, as much as the companies seems to be the bad guys, the consumers are as well, because if we were not to buy that crap they would not continue making them. Still, is it among us and nothing can change our situation today if consumers does not. Human beings are being brain washed and all we can think of is more, more, more, until what? We want more of this and more of that and a little bit of this and a little bit of that. We want every existing app in our phone, games, dating apps, training and diet apps and the list is an infinity. We want it all to simply escape our life and to simply escape important and meaningful conversations that could of been the solution to not ending your marriage, or to not break up with your loved one, to not loose your sick mother because of the lack of love and appreciation she got from you. We are all in this wheel of disruptions, phones and computers, iPads, we even start to read on a digital thing because "books is now not enough" anymore and we want something new, new, new. What we already have is ugly and useless. However, if you start to put your damn phone away, even just for a couple of minutes a day, and then hours and then maybe a whole day you will start to see a difference and you will start to not feel obligated to always check someone's post on instagram or Facebook, always checking your mail when your work shift is already over hours ago, always having the feeling of "I have to take a picture of this". I say NO, you really do not. Because it is the present moment that counts.

Does not matter how "instagram worthy" a picture is, let it be in reality and lets enjoy the present moment of watching that beautiful sunset or having the utterly loving and delicious dinner with your family or loved ones. Do not make your life being about your phone and all it includes. Do not let your life surround and depend on your phone and its content, it will bring you nothing but tension and restlessness. It will make you regret those moments you had because you were never really there, your phone was there, but you were never present and believe me, the people around you noticed and they would have wished for you to be there and be there with them, be there in their conversations, be there and feel grateful for even being able to be there. Be present among appreciative and meaningful moments, or even if it is just another walk, because all of a sudden it is not just walk anymore, it is a experience and something beautiful because all of the things you actually noticed when being present during your walk that you were not near able to experience when walking with your phone all the time, looking down on it all the time, talking with someone all the time, chatting, texting, emailing, taking photos and a list of possibilities in this little shit. Put your damn phone away, there is a whole world out there

and it is nowhere to be seen through a screen.
Put your damn phone away for you and your
loved ones.

33

To give but also to receive back. To show affection and love and appreciation by helping others, by running their errands, cooking for them, doing laundry and much more. To care and to show that you care can sometimes be the very most appreciative part of my day, however lately I recognise myself being the person who "does it all" almost and maybe I am taken for granted. Do not interpret me wrong, I love the moments when I feel like I am truly able to and really want to help one another because that is simply what I do and it makes me relieved and I feel comfort from doing it since I make someone else filled with joy. However, I can not be the only one among my loved ones to show this love and appreciation. There can never be too much amount of help and support in this world, however it can be handled wrong and some people may become other peoples "taken for granted" sort of person where the other person simply counts on me, on you just fixing and doing and helping without anything in return. To take someone for granted is to clearly treat someone with disrespect and with ungratefulness which someone is not worth experiencing, especially from someone you care about or someone you love very much. To me it is non comprehensible since it does not make sense and why would you not want to show love back? I have thought a lot of thoughts about this and I have thought about logical, reasonable reasons and causes which to me seems to be very common among a lot of folks, strangers too. I believe that people with too much going on, too much in within their schedules, as mentioned before, too much plans and that their "to do list" for the day is exaggerated and overrated, overestimated could be the true reason to people not giving back. All because, they always feel exhausted and tired, walking around in their own bubble with their egoism and doing whatever they want to do and whatever they have in their schedules, they do not care what your day looks like. They always take everything for granted and take you for granted and then it is not that odd that everything to them becomes meaningless and their eyes is only seen through their tunnel vision, seeing their path, their day, their to do list and nothing else. How come? Because they have such filled calendar and "nothing else matters because these are the things that are important", they say. They tell you they had a shitty day, a shitty week or

month or a year as an excuse of treating you
the way they do and it is a truly devious
behaviour that only comes from a self
absorbed, ego busy person only caring about
themselves. When noticing how one is taken
for granted you will feel very underestimated
and most likely forgotten and not loved at all,
because to love someone is to show it to them,
show it through words, appreciation, show it
by treating them with respect and helping
them reaching their desires. That is love.
Saying you love someone is simply not enough
and will never be to anyone because those
words have no meaning without constant
responsibility and taking action and doing your
best for both sides. Love is unpredictable and
unconditional but also very much seen when
two people or more show them utter
appreciation daily. To give and to give back. So
simple yet it seems so very hard. We must
remind ourselves that helping others and
showing our loved ones that we do care will
also make us feel good about ourselves and it
will bring you a sense of relieve and stillness. It
will bring you tens and tons of love back
because doing good means good will come
back to you and when that day comes we say
thank you and keep going with showing
appreciation to people whom we care about.
However, if the love is not coming back, then

leave wherever or whoever you are being present among, because it is not worth giving all your love to something or someone who takes you fro granted. Give people love but most importantly, make sure you get the love you deserve back.

34

To be absolutely empty with words, to feel stuck and limited and to have a feeling of not being able to let out one single word, to let out one single sentence at all. To feel deeply hollowed and to feel remarkably stuck. As I am trying to explain one of the many feelings I can feel during certain and specific situations, most commonly within family conversations and similar situations to them, I can sense teardrops in my throat and it feels hard to breathe. I feel overwhelmed. I feel overwhelmed by spoken words and unspoken words and pronouncements and expressions from people who I love and I do believe I sense a strong feeling of my heart aching this very day, this very morning writing at this very moment. I feel as if my heart got knelt down. I feel as if my heart were a piece of paper to just be crushed and thrown away and as if my heart were something to step on because suddenly it seems to have no value anymore. I feel overwhelmed but at the same time I am wondering about the very words being said and the feelings and emotions being heard, the expressions being expressed. When there is a

lot of tension, sadness, frustration and madness
going on in a room I really do want to stay
calm, I squeeze my hand and toes and my eyes
to not let my body get out of control and
certainly not my mouth with the words it
sometimes wants to just explode through my
voice. However I am not letting it happen
because I simply do not want to let it happen
and it is not how I handle such conversations
with such type of situation with overwhelm
and frustration. During this situation I find
myself truly listening to what people have to
say, I truly make an effort to deeply look them
in the eyes, let them know I hear you and I see
you, and also I listen to what you have to say
and yes I do in fact also care, very much, since
I love you and I care about you and whatever
is on your heart I want to know and I want to
help you and support you in the best way I
can. Because that is what I do and will always
do as long as you do it for me as well. This is
the point where I understood one very, very,
sincerely important part of this conversation. I
understood I did not receive the love back. I
did not even feel included at some parts.
However, I choose to interpret this in a way it
will not harm myself and I choose to keep
helping people because I want to and it makes
me achieve a meaning with everything and it
makes me get out of bed in the morning. I

want to help people and I want to write books. However, there is still a heartache speaking to me this morning and therefore I also choose to listen whatever going on inside me right now and in my head and what is going on with my thoughts and emotions right now and I will ask myself, what part of me will I let decide and be in charge for taking care of myself and protect myself right in this very moment? I choose my heart. I also choose to listen to my head and my thoughts and my emotions too, because they all play a crucial role to handle and process whatever got inside my heart during that conversation and whatever got stuck in my head. I glance at the window, all by myself at the kitchen table, holding my cup of tea, sitting up straight, breathing in and breathing out, closing my eyes, for 5 seconds, 30 seconds, 3 minutes… To simply be is the solution for me. To simply let whatever wants to be let out of my system. To simply be and let the stillness take control and to put my mind to ease. To handle such situations I choose to listen to my body, my heart, what is it trying to say and what sort of support does it need? I handle with stillness, communication with myself in utter peace and quiet with no one around me and yes that I make sure of, no one around me during this process of thinking or the last choice would be movement. To stretch my body, to go for a walk, preferably, to move freely in any way I feel like moving to sort of put by body into another focus and for my muscles to be in charge for a while so that my heart and mind can rest for a few minutes. I choose to handle such situations with caution and with a mindful spirit all by myself until I feel relieved and until I feel connected to myself again in a way I wish to feel connected with myself.

35

Some days, some minutes, some hours or even some specific months, there could be no feeling of being able to loosen up, to unwind, to calm down, to relax, to feel like you are actually on this earth and nowhere else. Today was the day. Today is the day where I believe my body is screaming at me and it wants to warn me, it wants to give me any type of possible, existing sign there is in this world. Specifically, for instance, the warnings that goes like this, "hey, do not go there", "you deserve better or maybe you do not", "I can sense and feel your pathway going in a direction this morning with your head in control and you are thinking wrongly, think again, because I am worried". I always choose to listen to my body and the very most insightful and instinctive thoughts appearing during my very walks every single morning at 6am where it sometimes frightens me what is about to be in my mind that morning, as for today. However, sometimes I feel very relieved and utterly empty of thoughts being marvellously peaceful inside. This is reality and this is existence and the art of being. However it is challenging and it is not much enjoyable when my body is trying to warn me from making a mistake or going somewhere I do not actually want to go. I trust myself but today I feel certainly lost and the real issue is who do I seek for help and support? I sure do have myself and I sure do believe in myself being my guide and personal comfortability, however during these specific moments there is more needed and I need guidance this morning. I believe there is to find guidance and support not only from having meaningful conversations with human beings but also to seek help from a different source of life, to me it could be going to church, to sit by myself, closing my eyes and listen to whatever silence has to offer and whatever answers comes to mind. I do also sometimes write down everything I feel and everything I question or feel hesitated about, anything I do not understand or comprehend, anything that comes to mind and anything I am wondering about and feel interested in knowing more about. I write it down because in some cases the paper in my book feel like the closest existing piece of life that helps me express myself in any possible way and in any way I want to express myself. To write on an empty paper makes me relieved and it makes me wonder why I even bother talking to humans sometimes. The paper gives all you need and it has all day for me to just be there and whenever I feel like writing I am capable of doing so and the paper is happy to help. During a lot of years I thought people were the only answer, "to always have someone to talk to", to always be with someone or otherwise I would seem lonely or suspicious, even ugly because I thought if I am not with somebody it means it is because I do not look attractive enough for someone to be with me, and yes this was present among me for a very long time and therefore the thought still shows up in my mind today, however I let it move on as the clouds in the sky. I acknowledge it and remember how I felt indeed, however I will not let it through me spiritually. I believed the people were everything, yet nothing and without people I would not be able to go through my day or even wanting to do so. Afterwards, a turning point appeared and suddenly people were the worst thing I could ever imagine being around and be having conversations with and to even look at. I truly hated the feeling of even be close to people and the eye contact were the scariest. I do really wonder why how one human body can feel such hatred and I do wonder why it even occurs that one can feel such way about human beings. I believe we were shaped and formed, developed and sort of forced to be in a certain way our whole childhood, from following rules that our parents made up, rules our teachers decided to include during school time, sports coach's rules, society's rules, unwritten rules. All of these limitations and to put people in the box seemed to be the most beautiful choice of them all. It is not weird that when you get closer to adulthood or even to the period of time when you are seen as a young adult, you start to think your own way and you desire to have your own beliefs and interpretations, wishes and dreams, goals and a routine that works best for you etc etc etc. However the world will not let you, because it seems like everyone is against you and utterly it seems irrelevant to even express yourself during class because all you get from the people in your class is laughter or a sense of nonsense words coming out of their filthy mouths which makes you even more afraid of being able to believe in your way o thinking and in your way of being. It came to mind during todays walk how we must not always surround ourselves around people, and if we do choose human beings it should undoubtedly be the ones who expresses outright with sheer honesty and respect, because the rest is for the mindless people with no heart and no touch of dignity at all. During this morning's walk I remembered and I felt my inner child being hurt and it truly hurt a lot and it also reminded me to erase what the teacher had told me, what my classmates from middle school yelled at me, what sometimes my loved ones used to comment on the way I look and the way I present myself, the way I was being. During todays morning walk I remembered myself of letting no one get into to my head because I will not let them and if they try again I will be damned prepared. My childhood is a part of me but it is not what defines me today.

36

Honesty. To confess, to be truthful, to give up all your lies, to show and express and let the words come from you and to stay fully you when telling your truth, the truth. I have come to conclusion that the simple and sometimes ugly yet treasured and useful honesty is our way to kindness, forgiveness and completion. We need to tell our truths, our inner truth to both ourselves and to the ones around us to even be able to call ourselves a person because not being truthful is to be living a fraud and to be having people carrying fraud among themselves. Because as long as the lies are alive within you and within your way of behaving you will start to surround yourself with people just like you who believes the lies win and that living a dishonest life will make you feel good and you will be able to run way from all your problems and that no arguments or fights will appear neither among yourself or with the people you are being around with. To disvalue the truth and to ignore the fact that it will only help you and nothing else is to simply put yourself in the shit and you will carry all of your loved ones with you if it becomes a habit and suddenly a very big part of your personality becomes you as a person; a liar. A fraud. Think about the person you will let down, the relationship that will most likely end, the marriage that will blow up and end immediately, you career collapsing all because of the fact that you can not be truthful to yourself and instead come up with all of these excuses, sometimes more of the minor versions such as, "sorry my bus was late", or "sorry I did not pick up our kids after school, I had some work to to do at the office", either that or maybe it was because you "accidentally" slept with your boss or even worse your boss's sister or even daughter, but why would that matter, right? Because it was only this time, and it will not happen again, and the teachers at school can handle my kids, no problem. And then you maybe come up with the feeling such as, "Also, no one knows about this so I do not have care at all or to be honest about it because it is too late, already happened. I will just carry on the way I have been". It could also be a scenario looking like this, "I know I promised to call you but I did not have time today and the rest of the week is kind of stressing me out right know", which could be a rather appropriate "excuse", however this one is about the fact that the person making this excuse actually do not want to meet this person at all and always come up with lame excuses to not have to meet her. When it comes to this point it is about the disability to not be able to face the facts, tell her you do not find your relationship valuable or meaningful anymore and would like to move on without this person. Because it ends up for the person always wanting to meet wasting their time as well. To make excuses untruthfully, and to being dishonest while making them up, such as in this situation, will make you feel atrocious, humiliating, you will feel like you let someone down and with utter disrespect since no one is to be treated this way, no matter who we are talking about, it is still a person with feelings, emotions, thoughts, beliefs and desires, just like you. You have no right to treat a person this this way and the only reason for you to treat someone this way is because of your disability to not share your truth nor to be honest with yourself which will hurt you and the person being lied to. To be truthful is to not have to carry this sack of stone on your back all day filled with shame and burden, it is about relieving yourself from those thoughts by simply telling your loved ones how you truly feel and to let them know you care about them, because that is what honest people do. They tell their truth and they are being honest so that they will not hurt anyone. To be able to tell the truth is to be able

to keep the most precious and meaningful
relationships there is to have and it will help
you keep those significant people and in return
they will stay truthful to you and always be
there when needed. To trust is not only to
trust, it is to give someone their whole self and
to rely on them with their life, it is to show
respect and dignity for one person in order to
be able to achieve loving and supporting
friends and relationships back. If you are
planning to continue living your lie, think
again and think of the damage it will cause to
you and your loved ones. Choose the truth and
the truth will guide you to utter satisfaction.

37

Are you aware of the feeling of true
excitement and warmth to something you have
been looking forward to or are looking forward
to? Have you ever felt the heartbeat going
insane and working as if it were a part of the
engines in titanic? Have you ever felt as if
today is THE day and today is different, it feels
different and I do believe, in my case today
really is different. It is not only an emotion and
it is not only I feel, it is something I know
because my hearts tells me so and I do listen to
what my heart has to say and the way it reacts.
I feel something relied today and I feel as if I
was all alone this morning walking, I was the
one and only single person on the street on this
earth to be present among traffic lights and
fresh air. At the same time I felt so thoroughly
connected to where I was walking, the ground
and I felt truly connected to the air I was
breathing and to what I saw and was looking at
all the time, buildings and bridges, lights and
trees, park benches and boats by the dock and
piers. Therefore I was alone among people
however I was present among the sky scrapes
and nature around me and I felt as if there is

so much we do not acknowledge and even take airtime to look at during the days when the streets are filled up with people and when the cafes and restaurant, buses and trains are invaded by human beings trying to get through their day with kids, work, grocery shopping and simply being without going insane due to all the fundamentally, s sometimes ugly parts of our society trying to make us more depressed, sad and anxious. Enough of that, enough of reality, today I focused on the small things and I reminded myself go them so clearly and very specifically, I took time to relay look at it all in front of me in my peace and quiet, all by myself and undoubtedly it was all looking delightful and dazzling. Because to simply pass by and ignore, take our reality, our society for granted will not only make it ugly but it will disappear as less attractive and less interesting, all because of the reason that we are seeing it as "just a building", "just a street", "just a traffic light", and even if that is completely logic and in fact true, it is not "just a building" or "just a traffic light", it is something to be fascinated by, who made it? What kind of people are being inside that building? What are they doing there? For what purpose are they, and specifically they spending hours and hours sitting in from of that specific computer? What could possibly be so interesting or maybe not so astonishing as the building look that they are doing all day long? It is alluring how our society works yet impossible to understand completely and since it is not really about knowing everything and for everything to make sense or have a reason, we could simply just be long our home, among our city or village, town or outside of town, wherever and however you live and to sincerely and without hesitation gaze at it like it is your home and nothing else. Your valuable home where all you need is to be found, loved ones, family and yourself with your heart in rate and your mind in focus. Use your intelligence as guidance and your heart as your closest and most useful element of your body to feel excitement and to understand what keeps your heart going. Your heart is in charge.

38

Sometimes I do not recognise my family.
Sometimes I do not recognise my siblings, my
parents. Sometimes I do not recognise their
behaviour or the way the speak to each other,
the way they look at each other, the way they
cooperate or do not cooperate with each other.
Sometimes, or more correctly, during every
single day I do not recognise myself.
Sometimes I do not recognise them and it gives
me a feeling of, "I do certainly not cherish this
feeling and I certainly am confused by its
turnover and by the fact that I do not
remember them the way I used to and I do not
identify my brother the way I used to identify
him. However, yes time is changing people and
yes things happen and yes there are probably
most likely reasonable reasons for this to
happen, and at the same time I do believe it
has to do more with me, myself than my
family. I do not feel like a part of my family
and I believe that is the reason. I acknowledge
them with confusion and disbelief, a sort of
grief and yet the truth is telling me, or at least
trying to tell me that I am changing in this
direction my family is not and I can tell by the

way I assuredly quite always seem to be sitting by myself not being included in conversations because I choose not to, because I am not captivated by the talk of watches and purses, trips and argues about what other people do and do not do, what they possess and not posses, what they are doing in their everyday lives and what they are not doing in their everyday lives. I believe I choose to not be a part of it, and no matter how deeply it surely catches me realizing I am saying no to my family, I believe there is a terrific reason for me to do so and to really feel the way I feel about them. By all means, I have come to conclusions and gotten enlighten, inspired, involved, bathed by another values, experiences, priorities than the material world which I can not stand. As much as I am beyond grateful and cherished to be born in the family I was born into, and as much as I love my siblings whom I grew up with and my parents who gave life to me, it is time to seek for my desires and since I believe there is more to explore within us then outside of us and I must do it with people whom inspire me and whom I can connect with for the purpose of letting myself thrive and letting myself be around people who can support my beliefs rather than make a fool out of me. I also believe our families and loved ones is our highest prioritise, however a family does not necessarily need to contain of birthmother and birthfather, a family is your home and a family supports you and love you unconditionally. Some day, you might have your own family, I might have my own family and we'll make sure to make it a home. A home for you and a home for your loved ones, wether that family consists of strangers, friends, siblings or the unknown.

39

Balance. Inner, outer and all there is in between. Chosen limits, chosen opportunities, chosen beliefs. A chosen balance flourishing everyday with a certain amount of this and a certain amount of that. A certain amount of peanut butter and a certain amount of sleep. A healthy amount of pleasure and a healthy amount of problem, good problems to be solved. A balance, truthful and complete. I believe there is a journey called life and I consider that life being about balance, more or less. How much of this or that we include in our lives and how much of this or that we accept and feel alright about being there or not being there. I suppose balance is our solution to a vigorous, various and dynamic life full of wisdom. We let our bodies and we let our minds and we let our souls be and do and at the same time we let those components get handled with regulations and relevant rules and we build ourselves a system that works particularly for us and primarily doing so for the long run, not just for the day or for the week, for the long run, for the advantageous. Before we were born, we were placed within

our mothers holy stomachs having no clue
where we were supposed to be put, then
suddenly we opened our eyes, saw a human
being, just like us, right in front of us and they
say "welcome to the world", or more correctly
putted "welcome to the hell son o a sphere
meowing you feel utterly confused, loved,
forgotten and appreciated at the same time. As
time passes by, years and days of learning,
making mistakes, being raised and surrounded
by rules from your parents and adults trying to
build you and prepare you for what our world
actually is about and how it works and how it
is cultivated. Being an adult later yourself you
come to your own conclusion, you must find
your own rules, limits and this sort of pattern
to live by and not those from previous human
beings, but rather from you and only you
making your own for your own good and for
your life to be experienced with independence
and intention. For your life to become yours
and not theirs or someone else's for that
matter. You will arrive at the destination
responsibility and the next destination called
self discipline and the next one self confident
and the train moves forward with a journey to
look forward to. Therefore there is no time to
sit down on the train looking out of the
window with chocolate bars in your hand and
a glass of whisky thinking everything will solve

itself and be alright just by sitting here. Indeed, have your whisky and chocolate bars but do not let your life be thrown into another humans hands and into another humans control and their rules by their limits and their balance, because it simply has nothing to do with you and their balance is not your balance. Their rules, their routine, beliefs and desires are not yours either. To find balance is to find aspiration and hunger for your soul to thrive and for your mentality to grow. It is for your inner child to heal and for your future self to not only regret what was before. To find your own balance is beneficial for your overall bloom and well-being. To find your balance is to find you and accept you and what you truly desire out of life and with help from having a balance within everything from a job, to family and pleasure it is not longer about strictness or unreal limitations, it will suddenly feel natural and comforting, therefore more delightful and gratifying days are allowed to be brought into your life. Balance is fundamental, start seeing it as fundamental and you will thank yourself for starting your real life journey; to find your balance.

40

At some points you may consider me telling you about crap as if I know how the whole world is functioning. The truth is, I have no clue and I have no clue sometimes what I am trying to tell you or me for that matter, what I man simply telling myself or what I am actually writing about, it just is there and it wants to be heard. However, one thing is for certain, I am not scared and assuredly, specifically not when it comes to having no clue at all, to not have right all the time, to make mistakes and to explain the world as I see it and preferably at some points that is the way you see it as well or perhaps wants to try and see it from another perspective. I am not here to change anything or to manipulate with words, however I do hope to give you and myself an alternative to how a human beings mind can be working and how a human beings habits and life can become beyond present and valuable to you. As I mentioned at the very beginning, this is not for you to read to just read or because you feel as you should rely on my or anyone's words because as I said before, what I believe must not be for you to believe as well, however it is to dare to think in a different way without being scared. I am not writing to be scary nor am I scared to write the things I choose to deliberate. I do not fear to be mistaken, to have doubts or to commonly be afraid of "losing an argument" just because that is the way the other people talking to me sees it. Fear and to be scared comes from how you see things and the way you look at the situation or the discussion, how you choose to clarify and illustrate and interpret something in that very moment when fear arrives upon you. To walk around being scared and worried and bothered about things that at the end of the day probably was not even that scary is to waste time and it will eat you alive, since it takes an enormous amount of time and energy to walk around tense and not loose at all. Funny thing is, this is me 150%, being scared is one of the most common feelings I feel, yet it keeps me alive, it is what thrives inside me and it is what challenges me and what puts me in positions to only become a better version of myself. It is not to lead you to your body walking around with the fight or flight feeling making you feel exhausted when coming home to "have to take care of everything because nobody else do and also my work sucks so I feel bad for myself, I should do nothing, just look at everyone else doing everything for me because I am so scared of everything and I can not face my fears". It is to lead you to development. SO, what are your fears? And why are they so scary? One might say they are afraid of talking to their boss about working less since they wish for more time for their health and for their family, but are too scared to face that discussion because one might look like a failure to their boss, a total mess and even weak to some people. Weak for what? Total mess for what reason? Failure? The only element to be considered a failure in this situation are the way you see your situation and the only one responsible for seeing it that way is you. I am not saying that you are a failure, but you failed the mission and you will keep failing unless you will see opportunities in your choices, a solution, an improvement for your family and for your health by simply facing that "awful" conversation and tell your inner mind to shut up sometimes, because feelings and emotions are hints and proposals of how you might be handling or thinking about the situation, but that does not mean it is the final conclusion of how to handle your fear. Do not believe me wrong, emotions and feelings are the most beautiful thing we own, according to me, however they are there to help you and to help you better understand the best options and ways to go by listening to them closely, and then in peace, not directly or instinctively rely on them, but to think about them very carefully and then consider the most relevant option that seems appropriate to you, not to the other part. In preference, rely on yourself being bold, because somewhere in our minds we get tricked and fooled, confused and distracted, most of the times those instincts arrives from the outside world, and the whole childhood trauma story to what one person may have told you today at work and it gets stuck in our system and therefore makes an excuse to not face our fears, to not be bold, when that is the only way to solve the whole situation. To face it and to deal with it, everything will go through the hard way and when starting to do it the hard way it may not seem so scary anymore, because that is simply how you become a lot more free from worrying and stressing around; to simply deal with it and to deal with it in the near future. Fear is not a part of your personality, rather it is a consequence from not dealing with what you are scared of. Deal with it and your boldness inside you will appear, and it will appear to help you.

41

Do not forget to breathe. Do not forget to slow down and do not forget to do this on a regular basis. During the day we shall be out of breathe as a result of putting our bodies in to work to benefit our whole system, but also we shall decrease and reduce every single activity going on in our bodies by simply slowing down and breathe so gently it will feel ridiculous and then you know you are doing it right. Breathe as if it were your last breath possible and do so with patience and softness. Breathe tenderly until your body feels numb and when closing your eyes you see nothing, it is all blank. The only thing supposed be around you and be present around you is the sound of your inhales and exhales and the very feeling of doing so. Feel your lungs expand and then dwindle, notice how your body reacts to its breathing, does it hurt? Is it painful? Do you feel as if your body is eased or do you feel like your body is loosening up? We shall let our bodies move during this experiment and we shall let hem move exactly how it wants to move. Follow your body today, you can not always be in charge of every movement it decides to take action to. We should give our head full of thoughts the approval to let it in to our body and to let our head experience this together with the rest of us there is. Perhaps it will feel strange, but hopefully it will light you up and as you breathe something lets go of you. Something, something, something. Just let it out of your system as you exhale and inhale with caution. I believe our breaths are the essential source of what comes in and out and therefore we should control our breathing as if our life depends on it, which it naturally does, however we seem to forget how to breathe and we seem to forget we are breathing. Remind you of the very fundamental and crucial function you have to live; breathing and do so with caution and honour.

42

When there is nothing to say, when there is literally nothing to say, I feel stupid. When in those moments I have nothing to say I feel so utterly powerless and weak and I feel as if my surrounding becomes empty and very very fragile. I feel as if it is ridiculous to be where I am and this is where my weak spot comes in and usually appears, namely, I want to run away, in these very moments I just want to run away and never come back. Over exaggerating? Probably. Am I doing it with willpower and without regrets? Of course not. However, where there are no words to say and when I feel as if my opinion does not even count or when my words are being stultified by someone, when my words are not words to someone, there are just insults and a way of attacking to someone when I feel as if I were not to tell people how I feel I deny myself and I deny the way I work and I do understand not to say everything that comes to mind because I would walk around looking like and sounding like a crazy person, so indeed, I will not do so. However, when it comes to having no words for the ones you love it deeply got to me that something is not right and I am certainly not comfortable with this conversation or situation at all. Having no words, and no words at many times these days and it must mean something, it must mean something is surely sucking the energy out of me and I am the only one responsible to take act on it and try to see a way out. I feel as if I were stuck in a kayak in the Amazon river not being able to get out of the water, drowning, slowly but rapidly at the same time and all you can feel is the pain in your chest and the demons swirling around in your head telling you, you will not make it you weak bastard because if you had solved your problems and issues you would not even be here at this moment. The truth hurts, it truly aches and it can surely torture one if it wants to and if one need to hear the truth maybe three or four times a day. The truth is also the way out and I know that. I know that so clearly and obviously it hurts even more and I am aware of the truth following me until I will be in action for it to be present in my head and for me to act upon the truth and let it help me instead of being scared of it. Speaking of being scared of things as we have been talking about in some previous chapter, yes, I am afraid of the truth and it scares me to death. It is without doubt a sort of love and hate kind of relationship since I have discovered my truth recently and it is fresh and fragile and outspoken, it is out there, it is present, it is legitimate and it scares me to death. The thing for me about the truth is that truth really is, it is just there and there is nothing you can do with it. You can not change it or like it or dislike it or ignore it or run away from it. It is there and will always be because it got brought up for a reason and I learned the hard way is the only way and also that it is suppose to hurt and it is supposed to take time to process and to accept and to value.

This morning, I have no words, and it feels dreadful and unpleasant, yet I believe in my truth and therefore this reaction is a part of my process of accepting it.

43

I often hear people talk about living your life fully and completely, to take huge risks and to live as if there is no tomorrow. I hear people all the time saying "you only live once", well no shit. Believe me, I have been there and I have done that and what I learned was mostly the fact that when living according to these measurements and instincts your life is always on the edge and you never know if you will ever see your family again or if they will ever want to meet you again. You never know if this is your last sunset or sunrise. This may sound extremely exciting and lovely at first and how astonishing it might be to live this way, according to a huge amount of people apparently. As you start risking and facing an infinity of challenges putting your life on the edge there is no going back and it will be terribly difficult to even see another possible life, because now all you got is a bucket list of insane activities as if you would want to kill yourself. As if the world only surrounds around you and your dreams and your achievements and your insanity where as your child at home is waiting for her mom or his dad to come home and read a bedtime story for the 500th time, because he or she needs you and there will always be someone who thinks you are important to them and to yourself but maybe you just did to realize it. It could plainly be a coworker who looks forward hanging out with you at work, the Liberian who always says hi to you when coming there to read, the girl at the coffeeshop who made you smile and you smiled back. It could also be your family, girlfriend, boyfriend, sister, brother, cousin etc. When I have conversations with people and they start talking about their next epic trip or the next extreme challenge or the next upcoming event which is about drinking vodka until you faint and end up in their neighbours pool outside, probably dying in that pool too, all I can really think to myself is; insanity. To live like this is to believe life should be lived extremely and to only include extreme events parts to your life and days because otherwise life becomes boring. This is the crucial part. To live by extremism is to confess that your life sucks and that you have no better way to spend your life than watching TV all day and eating bacon flavoured popcorn with a large coke. Or maybe you might have been cheated on or neglected by a friend previously and there it is; extremism. Brutal actions or a little less brutal actions such as watching TV and eating bacon flared popcorn with a large coke. The point is, we seem to always run away from taking care of ourselves and our lives. No wonder the extreme comes in since we want to feel alive, we want to feel as if there is no tomorrow because we can not simply bear the fact that there actually is a tomorrow and that we have to go on with our lives and take responsibility and action for change to happen. Extreme and brutal actions appears at our downfall type of days and it usually sticks for a very long time when starting to indulging it into our lives, since all of a sudden that seems to be the only "fun" and "meaningful" part of our lives nowadays, and also we make sure everybody is aware of it and we want to make sure everybody knows it so we spend the rest of our time and life on instagram and Facebook, twitter and snapchat, whatever shit you use, and put it all up there looking amazing and as if we have the time of our lives, when the very truth is, we are miserable and no matter how much we want to ignore that fact it is not possible. All because, everyday you will, hopefully, you never know when living like this, come home to your mess with takeaway Chinese food all over your sofa and empty beer bottles in your bed, maybe your bathroom too because you were too drunk to get up from the toilet and feel asleep with your beer in your hand. The point is again, to dedicate your life to life threatening actions and to think that there is no tomorrow, every singe day, is to already kill yourself and to kill your loved ones around, people who care. Therefore, we could talk about selfishness. You are not alone in this world and so do not act like you are alone, you do not only screw up for yourself but for the people who care about you and one day you will realize all you got is yourself and you madness and you will feel utterly lonely among it since it is insanity and people who acre about you have no interest in supporting you doing it. Wow, this reminds me of me months ago, still it happened. Also, maybe there is no tomorrow, but that is not up to you to decide, tomorrow will solve itself, today is important, and today is what matter. Today should be one day closer to solve struggles, problems and issues you are dealing with so that you can wake up to less problems and issues and struggles tomorrow. That is what it is all about, and to have food on your table of course. The fact is also that if you care about ore valuable shit, your problems will become more valuable to you as well and it will lead you to be wanting to solve them since they mean something to you. To live extremely will harm. To live with dignity and solve your valuable problems one by one will lead you to more valuable shit to deal with; simplicity over extremism.

44

Jazz. Lively and serene, gentle yet awakening. Jazz, jazz, jazz, how marvellous sounds it creates and how beautiful to listen to. Jazz, one of my substances to joy and creativity and tranquility. I listen to it everyday and I sure do adore the way it makes me feel and it just makes me want to move my whole body. Jazz lifts me up and when listening to it live I feel present among every single instrument and voice and sound and rhythm and base as if I were inside them when playing it. Last but not least, jazz is a new form of escaping, a rather healthy escaping to me, whereas I could just put that son of a jazz on and even for just 2 minutes feel more conscious and viable than I have ever being gifted before, for that I am pleased. Walking. The undoubtedly most astonishing movement of art possible on this earth. To simply move and let our legs be the engines in our body to persuade ourselves into thinking clearly and spiritually, which will guide and help and support us in the long run. I will walk until that day I may not have legs because that would surely and truly be the only reason for me not to be moving my body.

Listening. To sincerely and undoubtedly listen to me, listen to her or him, listen to what my body is trying to tell me, listen to what nature has to say, listen to the very environmental details around me every day; people, the sound of a bird, sounds from the very first drops coming out of my shower. I seriously believe listening have helped me find a stillness and peace and comfort when it comes to the fact that the world is so much more and everything does not evolve around me. Listening thought me new perspectives and I heard stories I have never witnessed before. I would like to thank jazz for being present among us these days. I would like to thank my body for being able to walk. Lastly, I would like to thank my ears for having the opportunity to listen and listen closely. Undoubtedly there is an infinite list of elements within my present life that I am truly and undeniably forever grateful and thankful for, however I choose to put and end to this book and so here it comes. The end.

the end

FEAR. Resentment. Destruction. Boldness, into RELIEF. Fulfilling. Development. Awareness. Presence. A ridiculous big amount of our world seems fucked up. That is just how reality is, and to admit that and discover a direction even though everything is fucked up, would be sincerely wonderful. All because, there is a life and light within you wanting to explore and expand, to grow and to be seen and heard, to be appreciated. There is a light wanted to be lit and a marvellous heart filled with tenderness and warmth within you ready to be your ultimate adviser when it comes to choosing what you love or what you may think you love. It is there to be appreciated and used. So use it.

You probably know me slightly, lightly, hopefully a teeny tiny bit better, and so we already know there is no "happy" ending because that would all be a distortion, and you know what I think about lies and how that makes one appear. There is our presence and our ability to being present which will ultimately and splendidly lead you to a statement of delight and gratification if you simply let it be your best mate and let it guide you into your biggest desires, whatever you desire from life and whatever you want to learn or teach, whatever there is for you out there waiting to be experienced. Everyday we should breathe, talk, walk, listen, interpret, feel, acknowledge, sense, simply be in the present until your mind feels empty and your thoughts seems inspirational and intriguing, until your body feels at ease from any tension or fear or anxiety stopping you from firmly anything in your way to be completely you and to be entirely existing and thriving. Our present is not something we take for granted, because that means living as if life itself should be taken for granted and that would be nothing but truly mistaken. Last but not least, choose your presence wisely and with respect to be able to fulfil and exist with significance; be beyond present with your own state of mind.